*TWELVE ANGELS FROM HELL*

*Other Books by David Wilkerson*

BORN OLD

GET YOUR HANDS OFF MY THROAT

HEY, PREACH . . . YOU'RE COMIN' THROUGH!

I'M NOT MAD AT GOD

JESUS CHRIST SOLID ROCK

MAN, HAVE I GOT PROBLEMS

PURPLE VIOLET SQUISH

REBEL'S BIBLE

THE CROSS AND THE SWITCHBLADE

THE UNTAPPED GENERATION

WHAT EVERY TEENAGER SHOULD KNOW ABOUT DRUGS

# TWELVE ANGELS FROM HELL

**David Wilkerson**

*with LEONARD RAVENHILL*

Lakeland

LAKELAND
116 BAKER STREET
LONDON W1M 2BB



*First Lakeland edition September 1966*
*Second impression November 1966*
*Third impression April 1967*
*Fourth impression October 1967*
*Fifth impression August 1968*
*Sixth impression November 1969*
*Seventh impression January 1971*
*Eighth impression October 1971*
*Ninth impression January 1973*

ISBN 0 551 00423 1
PRINTED IN GREAT BRITAIN BY ELLIOTT BROS. & YEOMAN LTD., LIVERPOOL

*THIS BOOK IS HUMBLY DEDICATED to W. Clement Stone and his wife, Jessie V. Stone, whose help, support and counsel have been a pillar of strength to Teen Challenge, to my wife and to me. This is but a small way to express thanks to this dedicated couple who are indeed blessed.*

## ACKNOWLEDGMENT

I honestly feel that I have invested the least of all in the writing of this book. I am author only in that my ministry has directly or indirectly influenced the lives of the "angels" whose stories are told here.

Much credit for the launching of this project belongs to Leonard Ravenhill, noted revival writer and evangelist, who suggested the title and helped get the actual work under way. Working together on this book has been a profound experience for both the Reverend Mr. Ravenhill and myself. We have gained a new appreciation for the marvelous grace and transforming love of our Lord.

We refer to these young people as "angels" only to signify the spiritual transformation they have all experienced. Their true stories are representative of many others like themselves. We do not suggest that they have finished their course. We present them to you as trophies of God's grace and they are displayed on these pages only to glorify Him and to inspire faith. We ask you to pray for them.

May God be glorified—may Christ be magnified—and may these patterns of grace encourage this generation to believe in miracles.

D.W.

*TWELVE ANGELS FROM HELL*

# 1

It felt good to be driving away from the city. New York was no place to spend a hot summer day, not if you had any reason to go somewhere else—and I did.

As I got closer to Pennsylvania a change began to come over me. I noticed a freshness in the air and decided to sample it, and as big, deep breaths worked down into my lungs I eased back against the seat. *Why,* I thought, *am I driving with my hands clenched so tightly around the wheel?* I relaxed my grip, and then I smiled. I went through these same exercises every time I headed for the hills.

I like any hills, but the rolling, generous Pennsylvania hills were pretty special to me for two reasons: Gwen and I had lived there for several happy years before we came to stay in New York—three of our four children were born there—and now, in those hills, some badly tormented boys were trying to learn that *life* and *hell* were two different words.

This was a good day to go to the farm. It was getting harder and harder for me to find the time to get out there, and sometimes when I did my mind sort of stayed on in Brooklyn. But today things were going well at the center. It was one of those rare times when old troubles were being tackled and new ones hadn't yet walked in the front door.

The day had begun right and I had a strong feeling that

it was going to continue that way—straight through to midnight. Sonny's letter had given me that feeling. My jacket was lying on the seat beside me, and in one of its pockets, neatly typed on a sheet of paper, was a miracle.

How right it was that I should get his letter on the day I planned to drive out to the farm and see how the new building was coming along. In a way, Sonny was a part of the farm, even though he had never seen it.

When I first saw Sonny, I wouldn't have believed he could ever be a part of anything fresh and green. Everything about the boy was gray, muddy brown, sickly yellow—he was the most haggard boy I'd ever seen. He leaned against a shabby building in a Brooklyn slum where very few people could afford decent clothes—and even there he was conspicuous.

He didn't seem to be aware of anything at the time—not the traffic or the torn dirty clothes he wore or the shoes that were falling apart. I couldn't help looking at him curiously because at first I couldn't tell whether he was young or old—but he didn't seem to notice me. He just stared ahead of him.

I was getting to know that section of Brooklyn quite well by that time, but I still couldn't accept the fact that teenaged kids could have such dark circles under their eyes, and pitifully hollow cheeks, and ugly brown remnants of teeth. I was always shocked—and I still am—to talk to people who look at least thirty-five, and later to find they are still teenagers.

Sonny was like that, only more grotesque, and the sight of him made my whole being ache for him.

"Can I help you, pal?" I said.

"Beat it." He didn't say the words the least bit forcefully—but he meant them.

"I want to talk to you."

Somewhere in those dismal eyes I thought I saw a spark flicker. "Beat it, fuzz." At least he moved—he turned his head and spat on the sidewalk, close to my shoes.

"I'm not a cop. I'm a minister." I was also pretty stubborn and it had helped me more than once when I was trying to get through to a street-toughened teen-ager. "Look," I said, "cops don't carry these, do they?" I showed him a small Bible I always carried in my pocket. "And they can't quote Scripture."

If I thought I was going to break down his resistance with my dramatic gesture, I was mistaken. Sonny was a master of indifference. "Get outta here, creep!" he sneered. "I've seen narco agents with them things—you can't fool me!"

"You've already been fooled, pal—a long time ago." I hadn't yet learned much about the more subtle evidences of drug addiction, but even then I could see that the boy was "high." And as long as he was, I'd never be able to help him. Even though I realized that, I couldn't let go. I felt so frustrated and I'm afraid I lost my patience.

"I'm not here to show you my credentials!" I snapped, putting the Bible back in my pocket. "I want to show you how to find a new life!" Then I felt ashamed. What kind of a life was I showing him—shouting at him? "I'm sorry, son," I said, and my hand went out to him. He didn't move much, but very distinctly he drew back in revulsion, as though I were the grimy one. He didn't have to say anything; I moved on.

I got to see more of Sonny as his neighborhood became a familiar beat in my street-corner ministry. At first I came to

New York only once a week, on my day off from pastoral duties in Philipsburg, Pennsylvania. Later, when Gwen and I were called to come and live in the city, I was able to give all my working hours to the troubled young people who lived most of their lives in the streets.

Sonny held back, and so did a lot of others, but gradually I was able to reach some of the teen-agers who were desperate enough to cry out for help. And they needed it, all right. Some of them were only thirteen, fourteen, maybe sixteen years old—and already they were alcoholics, muggers, prostitutes, addicts, even murderers. What kind of help do you give to kids like that? I gave them the only kind I knew.

"God loves you, Sonny," I said, whenever I spotted him, and he wasn't easy to miss. I usually got a snort in reply. "He really does. He loves you right now, the way you are, and He'd like to help you find a way out." Most times, if he responded at any length, it was with a snarl: "Kook preacher!" He had at long last stopped believing I was a narcotics agent.

Much as I wanted to get through to Sonny, I had to put my time where it counted for more. I had a message for street fighters, gang leaders, kids who stabbed each other with knives and jabbed themselves with needles—and a lot of them were beginning to listen. Wherever I could—in church, on a street corner, in a wretched abandoned basement that served as a clubhouse—I preached the message of God's love, Christ's atoning death, and the Holy Spirit's power to work wonders in this world.

I had begun with a somewhat shaky conviction that God had called me to work on those crowded, restless, lonely city streets. After all, I had been a country preacher for several years, and I sometimes thought I was awfully presumptuous to believe that God wanted me to make such a drastic change. But I saw enough miracles during those days to make me ashamed of my doubts. I saw more than one vicious, jeering, foul-mouthed young boy drop to his knees, shaking his head furiously to fight back the tears that seemed to force themselves out of his eyes; I saw more than one give way to the tears and then give way to God's love. I saw them rise, filled with new life, strengthened by new hope.

I was preaching in a church one night when I almost stopped talking. There he was, in the last row, slumped and dirty as ever—Sonny. I did stop talking, only for a moment, and said a silent prayer for him. I took another moment to remind myself that this was Sonny, the unreachable.

When the service ended I looked toward the back row. He was gone, and even though I knew better, I was disappointed.

Out of the corner of my eye I saw someone kneeling at the altar and I turned to him. Then I stopped, uncertainly. There, like a filthy heap of refuse, was Sonny, and he was sobbing.

I felt as though his sobs came from my own heart and I walked over to him quietly. I don't know how he could see me through the clenched fists he pressed against his eyes, but when I placed my hand gently on his head he said, "Hello, preacher."

"God bless you, Sonny," I said, and again I uttered a silent prayer, a prayer of thanksgiving.

I waited by his side until he could talk. Then I asked him, "What made you come here tonight?"

"You did—you told me to come."

"I don't mean it that way, Sonny. I always invite you to

come to church, but this time you made it. How?" I knew the answer. I had to make sure that he knew it, too.

Sonny's sullenness had disappeared. In its place was a wistfulness that was very sincere. But he was beginning to get annoyed with me again.

"All right, all right," he said, but not angrily. "You bugged me, preach. I started to believe what you said about changing my life."

"What about tonight? Why did you come here tonight? Was it just because you needed a fix?"

Sonny looked up, but not at me. "I need God, preach—I need Him real bad!"

I took Sonny home with me that night, and all during the ferry ride from Brooklyn to Staten Island I did a lot of praying—for both of us. I wasn't an expert on drug addiction, but something was telling me that Sonny would never be able to break his habit by himself. He needed more than my best wishes. He needed someone by his side through the terrible ordeal of withdrawal. But he needed more than just me.

We faced a cruel struggle, and I was well aware that addicts can do some desperate things when they want a fix. Would he rob me? Would he try to kill me? Gwen and the children were visiting in Pennsylvania, with her family, so I was not exposing them to immediate danger. But did I have the right to risk their future well-being?

Sonny wanted to move around, so we left the car and went up to the passenger deck. The night was slightly chilly but we sat outside. I looked at Sonny, sitting next to me on the open deck. He certainly wasn't an attractive house guest. Beads of sweat stood out on his forehead. Already he was feeling the cramps that mark withdrawal from drugs.

Now Sonny was beginning to doubt the reality of his conversion. He looked at me hesitantly when the ferry bumped and slammed its way up to the dock.

"Let's go, son," I said, and he followed me to the car.

During those days I lived in a small apartment that served as the only "center" of Teen Challenge. When the living-room couch was unfolded, we had room for one guest.

Sonny was fidgeting again by the time we got there so I filled the tub with hot water. I thought a bath might calm him down—at least it would remove some of the marks of his squalid past. I gave him a clean pair of pajamas and then I turned my attention to food. I was famished.

I tried not to look surprised when Sonny sat down at the table, but I didn't do very well. Frankly, I was curious. I had only the vaguest idea of Sonny's features, and even that came from guesswork. Now I saw that he had taken on color. Instead of being all gray and muddy and yellow, he was a blue-eyed boy with dark blond hair. His skin, still so pallid, had probably looked bright and healthy once upon a time. Maybe it could again.

I was so hungry that I gave all my attention to supper—until I noticed that Sonny hadn't touched his food.

"Would you rather have something else?" I asked him. "Don't you like soup?"

"It's okay," he said and picked up his spoon. He didn't put it into his bowl. I was trying to watch him without letting him know it, so I kept my eye on the spoon while I buttered another slice of toast. The spoon seemed to lose its way as it got near the bowl. It swayed a little in mid-air, then went down a bit, then up, then a little to one side; it made another start toward the bowl and then sank straight down to the table where it began to trace whirlpools in the plastic tablecloth.

I forced myself to finish my toast, although I wasn't hungry any more. I didn't know what to do—and I had to do something. I had taken an addict into my home and I was going to help him go cold turkey—now just how was I supposed to do that? First I had to get some help myself. "How, Lord?" I asked. "I don't have much time to learn. How?"

Sonny stood up and walked over to the desk. He tried to appear interested in the papers on it, but he couldn't concentrate. He was getting jumpy. Pretty soon he would want that fix.

Out of nowhere I got an idea that made no sense at all. "What do you say—let's go for a ride!"

It made sense to Sonny. "Yeah, yeah, that's what I need," he said eagerly, and he headed for the door.

I should have learned every inch of Staten Island that night, but it was too dark to see where we were driving. Besides, my attention was fixed on Sonny and I drove mechanically, up one street and down the next.

At first he seemed to settle down a bit. I thought I would keep up a conversation and possibly learn something about him at the same time.

"How old are you, Sonny?" I glanced his way, but he continued to gaze out the side window.

"Seventeen—I think," he muttered.

"Don't you know?" I tried to say it lightly, although I didn't feel that way.

"Sometimes I know. Sometimes I forget."

"Got any folks? Around here, I mean?" I had learned to

ask the question in two parts. So many of these teen-agers had parents who had abandoned them years ago, leaving them to the care of social welfare agencies and foster parents, sometimes several of them.

"Yeah, I got folks—my real folks." Sonny turned toward me. "Why?"

"Why not? Maybe they can help you."

"You sound like a social worker now, preach," he sneered. "I've got good Christian parents. They love God."

"They know you're hooked, then?"

"How dumb d'ya think they are? They didn't know when I started, no. But you start using the needle and people start to notice things." He shifted in his seat.

"Don't they want you to kick the habit? Did they ever ask you to try?" Usually such questions were futile. If teen-age addicts had any parents at all, they rarely did more than throw up their hands or throw the kids out.

Sonny's parents were different, apparently. "*Ask* me?" he laughed. "They all but broke my arm to get me to go to that place—you know, that federal place."

He meant the Federal Hospital at Lexington, Kentucky, where addicts can go for treatment. There they are brought through withdrawal gradually, with the aid of carefully administered drugs and a program of psychotherapy—over a period of months. Then, when their records are stamped "HTC" (hospital treatment completed) they are sent home by train. Their "cure" usually lasts until they locate a pusher —and that often happens right on the train!

"Did you go to Lexington?" I asked Sonny.

"Sure. Sure I went. It did me a lot of good." His mouth was almost a sneer. "You know what, preach? They dried me out and when I got my first fix after that, it was almost as good as the first time I ever used the needle."

I was sorry I asked him so many questions. The appealing wistfulness that had come over him in church was gone and I was finding it harder and harder to reach him. I began to wonder how I ever thought I could help a boy with a problem as big as Sonny's. I was only beginning to comprehend its size and already I was crushed by it. How would I feel if I had to carry it on my shoulders?

Sonny's laugh jolted me out of my thoughts. This time it was a real laugh, with a little fun in it. "You're okay, preach," he said. "I was just rememberin' how I thought you was a narco guy. I sure musta been high that day!" I was so relieved by his sudden friendly manner that I joined him, most sincerely, in a laugh.

A few moments later I thought I would never laugh again.

Sonny was doubled up in the back of the car, drenched in sweat, and twitching in unbearable agony. He was going cold turkey, and I will never forget how I learned what the strange term meant.

I made a U-turn and drove back to the apartment as fast as I dared. As soon as I could get the couch opened up I put Sonny to bed. His legs jerked violently and beads of perspiration soaked his pajamas. One moment he shivered from a cold feeling, and the next he threw back his covers trying to shake off hot flashes that apparently burned like a fever. "Goosebumps" which made his skin look like that of a dressed turkey were visible all over his arms and neck.

As I watched helplessly Sonny rose up on one arm and spoke apologetically. "I hope I don't ruin your clothes or spoil your rug. Maybe you made a mistake taking me in like this."

"I didn't make any mistake," I said.

I picked up my Bible and began to read from Psalm 31.

*In thee, O Lord, do I put my trust;*
*Let me never be ashamed:*
*Deliver me in thy righteousness.*
*Bow down thine ear to me; deliver me speedily:*
*Be thou my strong rock, for an house of defence to save me.*
*For thou art my rock and my fortress;*
*Therefore for thy name's sake lead me, and guide me.*
*. . . for thou hast considered my trouble;*
*Thou hast known my soul in adversities;*
*And hast not shut me up into the hand of the enemy. . . .*
*Have mercy upon me, O Lord, for I am in trouble: mine eye is consumed with grief, yea, my soul and my belly. . . .*
*My strength faileth because of mine iniquity, and my bones are consumed. . . .*
*Make thy face to shine upon thy servant:*
*Save me for thy mercies' sake.*

I knelt down by the folded-out couch and prayed. I knew that Sonny was listening as he became quieter and I cried, "O Lord, stop his pain. Set him free and make him clean. Show him Thy power and fill him with the Holy Spirit."

I never thought I would sleep that night, but when Sonny fell into a fitful sleep I could no longer keep my eyes open. I was disturbed by all sorts of frightening probabilities and most of them were well founded. When an addict wants a fix badly enough, he will steal anything he can carry and sell it for whatever he can get. My room certainly wasn't a treasure house, but he might have made off with my radio or my wristwatch, maybe even my suit and coat hanging in the closet.

I must have carried those thoughts into my sleep because I suddenly sat up, knowing I had heard something yet not sure what it was. There it was again. Someone was moving along the wall, near the kitchen.

"Is that you, Sonny?" I called, knowing very well that it was.

He must have stumbled into something. I heard a thump and a curse.

"Sonny," I said, trying to sound very calm, "do you want something?"

"I'm hungry. I want something to eat," he said and then I blinked as he opened the refrigerator door and the bright morning light shone into my eyes.

I closed my eyes, but not against the light. I wanted to pray some words of thanks before I got up to fix breakfast.

I was only five miles from Rehrersburg and the farm, and I realized that my reminiscence of Sonny had made the trip very short. Yes, I thought, if we had had the farm then, we might have saved Sonny from a lot more pain.

An addict doesn't go through cold turkey and come out of it cured. Withdrawal, without the aid of medication, lasts for an average of three days. It means that the addict stops taking narcotics, and while it is the roughest, most drastic part of a cure, it is also the shortest part. Narcotics addiction has both physical and psychological aspects, and the physical part of the habit can be broken during the period of withdrawal. But the psychological aspect of the habit—the mind that has been hooked—may require years of treatment.

All this I had to learn, step by step, addict by addict—and Sonny was one of my teachers.

I stayed by Sonny's side for two more days and watched him—frail and battered—fight his way back to reality. I found myself praying for him, more and more, and as I did my feeling of helplessness began to melt away. Sometimes, in less painful moments, Sonny knelt beside me and prayed too.

He told me his story in bits and pieces and I found that it was very similar to those I had heard from some of the street-corner converts. His exception was his parents. Apparently they had tried to keep a good home for Sonny and his little sister and had even moved from their old neighborhood when they saw it was running down. They tried to keep their children from joining gangs in the street and wanted to bring them up in the church, but somehow the new neighborhood began to run down too. Pretty soon the teen-agers began to band together in vengeful gangs, and those who wouldn't join became their victims.

Sonny got tired of being beaten up on his way home from school. He began to play hooky from school—and from church school, too. It was all right for his folks to go to church and mouth all that religion jazz; they were getting old, and religion was good for old people. The gang—the club, as he called it—was the thing for him. He never got beaten after he joined—at least, not by anyone in his own neighborhood. Sometimes he got hurt when his gang went to war with a gang from another neighborhood, but that was different. It gave him a certain distinction. He was a wheel—especially if he had done some damage to the enemy.

He learned a lot through the gang. He went from cigarettes and alcohol on to marijuana and heroin just as some boys go from short pants and shrill voices to long trousers and electric shavers. They were the marks of his maturity, that's all, and he was never going to get hooked on the stuff—not him! How often I was to hear that vow!

"I wasn't hooked, even when I took a fix every day," he told me. "I had it under control."

"Sure," I said, "as long as you could get your hands on another fix."

Sonny looked away. "Yeah, you called it. It got to be more than one fix a day, and one day I ran out of money. I was hooked, all right. Man, I twitched! I shook all over. I didn't know what happened to me!"

"What did you do?"

"What else? I got a fix—fast!"

"How? You didn't have any money."

Sonny hung his head. "I stole it. My mom came home from work and I didn't want her to see me that way. She didn't know yet—about the habit. I hid in my room until she went in the kitchen. Then I grabbed her pocketbook and ran."

My heart went out to that woman and the anguish she must have felt when she began to put things together.

"Did you go back home, Sonny?"

"That night. I was pretty high. I don't remember much."

"What about your mother and father? What did they do?"

"They tried to take me to church. Then they tried to take me to a doctor. I wouldn't go—not to anybody. They cried, both of them, real hard. But what could I do? I needed another fix."

Sonny didn't stay at home. He began to sleep in flop-houses, in doorways and cars—anything that was cheap. His habit got more expensive and he had to steal to support it. Finally the police began to pick him up, searching him for narcotics, and Sonny was scared. That was why he went back home to his parents. He knew he needed help. They persuaded him to apply for treatment at Lexington, and when he managed to get his "HTC" their hopes soared. How cruelly they crashed to the ground when he got off the train and they saw he was high!

I wanted to go and see Sonny's parents when he began to come out of withdrawal, but I didn't want to leave him alone. I had another reason for wanting to get back to Brooklyn and I hoped he might be interested enough to come along with me.

"Want to go to Brooklyn with me today?" I asked him. Three days had passed since we went for that unforgettable ride and Sonny was beginning to regain his appetite. He had eaten a big breakfast and enjoyed it.

"What for?"

"I'm looking for a house. Thought you might want to come along."

"You kidding?" His eyes narrowed slightly. "That costs money."

"I know. It'll come when I find the house. But I might need your advice about a house when I find it."

"Why? What do I know about a house?"

"Sonny—." I hesitated. Maybe it was too soon to put a

vision into words. No, that was foolish. The vision needed not only words but action.

So I told Sonny about the center I wanted to open. A center for boys and girls who were lost—lost in all kinds of trouble, sin, despair. I wanted to open a house where they could recover from the wounds of hate in the world, a house where they could be healed by God's love. I had seen enough of these so-called delinquents to know that their crimes were the symptoms of their misery. They were responding in kind to a world that had no love in it. They were trying to stomp each other because their world had been stomping them since the moment they were born.

"How're you gonna find this house, preach?" Sonny asked, and from his tone I knew I had aroused his interest.

"I'll get a sign. Maybe not today, or tomorrow, but when I find the house, I'll know it's the one God wants us to use."

"Pretty sure of yourself, aren't you?"

"No, Sonny, not at all. But I'm sure of God."

The water was very choppy that day and we could feel the ferry pushing its clumsy, massive way through it. Again we sat outside on the deck, but it was daylight and I had a good chance to see the change in Sonny's appearance. I had bought him a pair of slacks, a shirt, and a windproof jacket to replace the clothes I somewhat victoriously put in the incinerator, and their newness matched the bright, alert expression that had recently come into his blue eyes. The dark circles were fading rapidly and his cheeks were less gaunt. The breeze blew his clean blond hair straight up in the air.

As we pulled into the dock I noticed that Sonny's hands

were restless. He kept jamming them into his jacket pockets and pulling them out again, over and over. I decided not to add to his tension by mentioning it, but when we drove off the boat onto the dock he seemed calm again and I heaved a silent sigh of relief.

It started again as we drove through one of the poorer sections of Brooklyn. His hands went in and out of his pockets. I was trying to keep one eye on him and the other on traffic, hoping I would have to stop for a red light. Every light was green. I felt I had to say something, but he beat me to it.

"It's no use, preach," he turned to me with frightened eyes. "Can't say you didn't try." He reached for the door handle.

"Sonny, wait!" I stopped the car, right in the middle of traffic, and immediately I was almost drowned out by blaring horns. I seized his arm. "If you got through these past three days, you can go all the way. Don't give up, Sonny!"

"Look," he said in a low, fierce voice, "you been real good to me, and I know you mean it. I think you really believe all that stuff about God and love—you sure treated me decent. But I gotta get a fix!"

"Then ask God to help you—He will! He wants to!"

He pulled my hand off his arm. "I don't think I could hurt you, preach—I couldn't even steal from you. But don't try to stop me."

I had the feeling that I was witnessing a deadly struggle for a boy's soul. It was a battle between the Holy Spirit and the spirit of evil and I could see the painful clash of combat in Sonny's eyes. The horns blew long insistent blasts and the drivers behind us shouted out their windows, yet somehow they seemed very far away. All I could hear was the sob that came from Sonny as he jumped out of the car and ran down the street, never looking back.

I pulled into the road leading up to the farm and stopped the car. The memory of that day had shaken me and again I reached into my jacket for the letter. Yes, it was there.

I remembered having a similar feeling of puzzlement when I heard about Sonny again, almost a year after he had fled down the street. By then my dream had taken on more than words and action. It had become a spacious and beautiful brick house on a tree-lined street in Brooklyn; and under the name of Teen Challenge Center it was becoming known among teen-agers as a center of hope.

The Holy Spirit doesn't give up the fight just because He loses a battle. He continued the fight for Sonny until He won. And one day Sonny showed up at Teen Challenge. I wasn't there that day, but Billy was and he told me about it when I returned at night.

Billy Martinus, one of my most trusted fellow workers, had once led an existence that seemed in its way more hopeless than Sonny's. Pushed out of his large family's one-room apartment and into the streets at a very early age, Billy had had an almost insane craving for cruelty. He got a thrill out of hurting smaller children, enjoyed toppling anyone on crutches; once he had pushed a blind man in front of a bus. Billy joined the notorious Mau Mau gang, and became such a wild fighter that although he led their rumbles, the rest of his gang never dared get very near him in a fight; they were never sure whose ribs his knife would enter next. He had been in jail twelve times and was plotting the murder of a rival gang member when the Holy Spirit turned Billy right side up. Now Billy had attended Bible School and was becoming more and more a right-hand man for me.

Billy told me how Sonny had been hearing about Teen Challenge, how he began to run into people who found help there. Some of them Sonny had known as addicts, hooked as badly as he, and they had kicked the habit. Not only that—a change had come over them, something he couldn't explain, but something familiar. Something else was familiar—that name of the director, Dave Wilkerson. Sure, the preacher!

"Are you sure this is the same boy, Billy?" I couldn't quite allow myself to rejoice yet.

"Of course. He remembered you. He told us all about the time you tried to help him. He said you really did get to him, too."

"But didn't he resist you?" I couldn't picture Sonny coming to Teen Challenge on the first invitation.

"Resist? That's not the word for it!" Billy laughed.

"It took three of us to break him down—and he knew one of us as an addict not so long ago! Sonny used every excuse in the book to avoid us, but we kept after him."

In a clean warm room down the hall Sonny was going through cold turkey again. Since the days on Staten Island he had been through it many times in barren jail cells, lying on the cold floor, kicking his legs in pain, and grimacing up into the glare of a light that never went out, night or day. Each time he had vowed he would never get hooked again, and each time he came out of jail thinking of only one thing —his first fix.

"He's going to make it this time, Billy. I think he's ready now for God."

Sonny made it, all right, and he stayed on at the center for quite a while. Like Billy, he was able to reach out and pull others away from the brink of hell, patiently going back for them again and again. He knew what it was like to cower on that burning edge.

I missed him when he went to California, but I couldn't have been happier about his reason for going. He had found a new life, and he wanted to give it to God by helping others who were lost. He was ready to begin Bible School.

The letter that had come in the morning mail was not the first I had received from Sonny since he enrolled at La Puenta Bible School, but it was the one that convinced me that a miracle had unfolded—slowly, step by amazing step—in his life. He had had some trouble with his courses at first, which wasn't surprising for a boy who had played hooky so much during his school years, but it put a great strain on him, and I wondered whether he could handle it. He had seemed a little shaken by it in a previous letter.

But only that morning I read the words of a boy who had found that God's love brought him a lasting strength. *I'm okay, now, Dave,* he wrote. *Maybe I have to study a few more hours than most people here—but I've spent time in worse ways than that, haven't I? Besides, I'll really know what I'm saying when I tell some kid to go back to school and learn something.*

We could do a lot more for boys like Sonny now that we had the farm. I drove up the road eagerly, trying to look past the big white barns to the foundation of the new building up ahead. But I have a soft spot in my heart for barns, especially when they shine with the luster of fresh paint, and I slowed down. The deep bass voices of the cows in the dairy came as teasing reminders that no matter how long I had lived in the city, I was still a country preacher—and there, in the middle of rounded hills of grass and grain, I had a grim realization. I could sing out loud when the hills welcomed me home. What about boys whose roots were in the cement and asphalt of crowded cities? Suppose they did get away to a farm for a few months, even for years? What happened when they went back to the city? Surely familiarity made claims on them—but where I could feel it as a welcome embrace, would they feel it a stranglehold?

A sudden sense of urgency made me drive faster.

"Hey, Dave!" The boys called out to me as I pulled the car to the side of the road. Some of them dropped their shovels and came to meet me, wiping the perspiration from their foreheads as they walked.

"Hi!" I called. I took my time getting out of the car because I was always very moved when I saw the changes that took place in these boys after they had spent some time at the farm. They walked with energy in their steps, and their tanned faces seemed to reflect the sun. Laughter was part of their vocabulary.

"Brother Reynolds said you'd be here one of these days," Jimmy said. "Good to see you." He held out his hand to me and his grip was firm. It was hard to believe that his close-set dark eyes, now almost merry in their brightness, had only recently looked out at the world with an animal ferocity. And Jimmy had lived up to the look in his eyes. Eventually he added to it a nose that was broken too many times to mend properly.

One thing we couldn't change, and neither could the warm rays of the sun. Under the tan on his arms I could still see the dark lines where healthy veins had once been. He would have those scars for life.

"How are things going, Jimmy?" I asked.

"Great!" he answered, and there wasn't time for anything more. I was surrounded by proud, happy boys who wanted me to look over the work they were doing. Under supervision they had helped dig the foundation for the new building and they intended to take on a lot more of the construction work.

I looked over the foundation very carefully and I began to share their pride in it. "It's wonderful, fellows. I mean it—this is the best work I've ever seen."

"Well, we're a little slow—but we're catchin' on now," Jimmy said.

"We'd better," Victor joked, "or we'll have to sleep on the grass when some new guys come up." Jimmy didn't laugh. In fact, the remark seemed to bother him.

I mentioned this when I talked with Frank Reynolds, our farm superintendent. Frank is a dedicated minister who always finds time to learn what makes each boy tick. Many young addicts owe their lives to this wonderful man and his staff.

"Maybe I'm picking at straws, Frank," I said, "but Jimmy seemed to be bothered by that remark. He just picked up his shovel and went back to work."

"I know," Frank said. "He's been asking me a lot of questions lately about how long we let the boys stay on here."

"What makes him think there's a time limit?"

"Nothing here. Maybe it's something inside him."

Everything else was going so well that I had no excuse to over-stay my visit. Before I left I stopped in to say goodbye to Jimmy. He was in the dormitory, a large, cheerful room full of daylight that streamed in from several windows. The beds were neat, and the covers were clean and colorful.

Jimmy was cleaning out a drawer in a table by his bed and a letter was lying on the floor. I picked it up and recognized the handwriting. It was the same carefully lettered script that I had first seen on a letter addressed to me a few months ago. "My boy has been in prison. He is getting out. He has no place to go. We can't do anything with him. Please help him." The letter came from Jimmy's mother and the short, choked sentences somehow brought the sound of crying to my ears.

"How's your mother?" I asked as I handed him the letter.

"All right, I guess." He put the letter in the drawer, out of sight.

"Do you want to see her?"

I was surprised by the anger that lit up his dark brown eyes. "You wanta get rid of me, preacher? You wanta make room for somebody?"

"Jimmy!" He was extremely agitated and I put my hand out toward his shoulder. He flinched—something he hadn't done in a long time. "Sit down," I said, as gently as I could. He sat stiffly on the bed. I sat on another bed across from him but he wouldn't look at me. "All right, what makes you think we're pushing you out?"

"Just tell me one thing—how long can a guy stay here?"

"As long as you want. Has anybody been pushed out while you've been here?"

"No." His arm shot out toward the drawer and he picked up the letter and waved it at me. "Can I go see my mother?" He flung the words like a challenge.

"Of course you can." I spoke very slowly because I was

trying to listen for the plea beneath his words. Very rarely could one of these frightened kids come right out and put his fears into words. But sometimes the hurt within them was so deep and so big that it had a voice of its own.

Jimmy stood. "Yeah?" He braced himself defiantly. "And I get to come back?"

There it was—the plea.

"Sit down Jimmy," I said again, and I was a bit surprised when he did. "Now, if you want to go and visit your family, go ahead. You can stay at the center in Brooklyn if you want." His eyes narrowed and I leaned forward. "When you finish your visit, you can come back here."

Jimmy lowered his head and I couldn't see his face, but I think he understood. "We didn't try to keep you with us when you came to the center, did we?" I asked. He shook his head. "Okay. And we're not trying to push you out of here. If we were, we wouldn't be needing that new building."

On my way to the car I remembered that Jimmy certainly didn't intend to stay long when he first came to Teen Challenge. He thought he didn't have much choice about coming. His mother had pleaded with him after she wrote to me and I had visited him while he was still in jail, inviting him to come to the center when he got out. I also got a lot of help from the prison chaplain and the probation officer. They began to put pressure on Jimmy before he was released, and they had good reason. He was a mainliner, an addict who injected heroin directly into his veins, and he had spent more time in jail than out of it. It was only a matter of time before he got into trouble that might cost him his life, or what was left of it.

We knew that Jimmy was trying to humor everybody when he agreed to come to the center. Just to be sure he got there, two of our workers met him at the jail on the day he was released.

"Okay, okay," he said, in his clipped, jittery rhythm, but his eyes darted past them. He was looking for a pusher. "What d'ya got for lunch?" he quipped.

Jimmy didn't get lunch right away. He arrived a few minutes before a service in the chapel, and immediately I saw that he thought he could use the center for a bed and a meal ticket.

"First we'll go in the chapel," I said and headed for the door.

"What for?" he growled indignantly.

"To pray."

"I can't pray on an empty stomach!"

"Well, that's the only way you'll get it filled," I told him. "Around here we pray the food in—and anything else we need, too!" Jimmy was so stunned that he followed me into the chapel and I could feel his eyes on me as I knelt to pray. I wasn't the only one on my knees, either. There were other kids praying, too, and Jimmy could see that they were his kind. His wasn't the only broken nose, his weren't the only needle-scarred arms, his wasn't the only heart that had never been warmed by love.

Jimmy had to be reached quickly or we'd lose him. He wasn't the kind who would give us much of a chance and he certainly wouldn't come back again once he went out the door.

He didn't know it then, but I was praying very hard for him, praying that he would feel the presence of Someone Else in that chapel. He did.

I felt the impact of his body as he sank down beside me with a long, low moan. I began to pray aloud that Jesus would come into Jimmy's heart and fill it with His love. I prayed, too, that the sobs of the shaking boy beside me meant that he was willing to give his life over to God. Only through surrender could that miserable soul ever look up in triumph.

I felt a hand on my arm. "What gives, preacher?" Jimmy rasped and he ducked his head angrily to wipe his tears on my jacket. "What's goin' on in me?"

"*God* gives, Jimmy!" I held him by the shoulders and he had to look at me. "He gives you love—a new life—a chance to change everything that's been hurting you, killing you!"

He was shaking and I dropped my hands. "All you have to give is yourself! Reach out and take His hand—He'll never let go!" Jimmy reached out, and he held on—at least he had until now.

I was accustomed to suspicion. Most of the kids who came to us had been used, tricked, and cruelly deceived all of their lives. It wasn't strange that most of them suspected us of running some new kind of racket. We knew that they had to overcome their own doubts, but we worried when they put us through their crafty little tests—because they were also testing themselves in the process, and some of them weren't ready for it.

Sure, Jimmy might want to find out whether he could leave the farm—just as we had said he could—and still come back to it. But he would also be subjecting himself to the temptations of his old neighborhood if he went to visit his mother, and he hadn't been away from it for very long. Physically he was a new boy, but he had not yet been baptized by the Spirit and he was still spiritually weak.

"Hey, Dave!" I heard a voice from somewhere over my head. I turned and saw Jimmy leaning out the dormitory window above me. He was smiling. "I can't go back now, Dave. I gotta work on the new building."

"Okay, Jimmy. We can use you," I called back.

"Maybe later on. Maybe in a couple of months."

"Any way you want it," I said, and he disappeared from the window.

My car was parked in approximately the same spot where I had stood talking with Arthur Graybill only two years ago. Then, too, it had been late in the afternoon and we turned our backs to the brilliant summer sun. I looked around at Arthur's 200-acre farm, rich with the yield of summer, and I could see the spiritual harvest Teen Challenge might reap if we could only find the money to buy this beautiful land.

I felt then that this was the place where God wanted us to build a rehabilitation center for boys who were ready to do something important with the new lives they had found. Still, I couldn't be sure that I wasn't being strongly influenced by the beautiful scenery. I had to find out.

I broke a twig off a young tree that was just beginning to run with sap and scooped away a handful of rich brown earth at my feet. I guess Arthur was a little puzzled but I had forgotten he was there and didn't bother with an explanation. "God," I said, "this looks like the right place to me, but I want to be sure it's what You want. There are a lot of boys who want to get to know You better, but it's not easy to do it on those hot city streets. They know You're there all right, but they know a lot of other things are there, too, and they've never had a chance to get away from them."

A soft breeze tugged at the twig in my hands, and I

pressed it into the earth. "If this is the place where they can come to learn about You, then give us the means to buy this land."

I had followed God's calling from the Pennsylvania hills to the New York City slums and I had had many doubts along the way. But every time I asked God to confirm something He wanted me to do, He always did. Once I knew I was going in the right direction, I didn't worry about how I was going to get there.

God wanted us to have that land, and Teen Challenge received the money to buy it. It came in shortly after I knelt in prayer by the little twig. All of our money comes in answer to our prayers. It comes from churches, foundations, from the pockets of teen-agers all over the country.

Sometimes we wonder how we can dare to go ahead and negotiate for a new building, or recruit new student workers when our bank account is always so low, but we do it, anyway. Somehow the money comes in when we need it, and more than one donation has been accompanied by a letter explaining that the donor learned of our need and somehow "felt moved to help us."

By the time I saw New York's audacious skyline on the horizon it was getting dark. Lights were going on in the tall boxes of buildings, and they had been switched on for some time in the oncoming cars.

The constant brightness of headlights flipping past my eyes made me feel tired from the hours of driving and I gave way to a yearning for home—I was, after all, becoming enough of a city boy to call it "home."

I told myself that there probably wasn't any need to look

in on the center before dinner, but I knew I would go anyway. I had two speaking engagements on my calendar for the next day and I might not get the chance to go to the center at all. That bothered me—and I realized that I was bothered a lot lately by anything that took me out of town. Oh, well, I told myself, you won't be going out of town tomorrow, at least. I was going to speak to two local churches and we needed their support.

No matter how bright the streetlights, the slums always look dark, dingy. The center was on a street that was an island of neat respectability, but on impulse I took a left turn instead of a right and headed toward the docks.

The buildings on each side of the street were favored by the darkness, for their dilapidated condition was somewhat hidden. Still I felt that they reflected the shame and humiliation of the people who lived much too close together inside their damp, decaying walls. I knew that long, long ago they had been built as row houses, but during the day the buildings seemed to huddle close together to keep out even the smallest crack of daylight. These streets, once a neighborhood, had become an area—which in New York City means that no one knows quite what to do with them. The best the inhabitants could hope for was that a bulldozer might appear on the streets one day and they might have to scatter away from its path.

Scarce as space was, now and then I saw what might be considered a lot jammed in between two buildings that seemed to try to squeeze it out of existence. No grass grew there but garbage flourished. Thrown from windows above, all kinds of refuse lay in the dank patch and gave off a rancid odor. In one lot I saw a pasteboard Halloween pumpkin—it had been leering toothlessly out at me for the past year.

This was where violence-hardened teen-agers were supposed to throw away their knives, dismantle their zip guns, and dump their needles in the river. How could they understand the meaning of love when they lived in a place that flew the banner of hate?

A well-meaning social worker had aimed some rough criticisms at Teen Challenge a few weeks ago and I had given them a lot of searching thought. It's not that I'm sensitive to criticism, but some of his questions had been popping up in my own mind.

"What about these kids you claim to have helped?" he said angrily, pointing his finger at me from across the room as he paced. "Where do they go from here? To a farm? To a school, maybe? I don't see them back on their old streets!"

Anyway, he was accurate. No, we didn't encourage teen-agers who had kicked the habit or left the gang to go back to their old haunts. Most of them didn't want to go back. Most of our success stories were about boys and girls who sought a new environment after finding a new life, and I sometimes wondered whether this was a sign of weakness in our program. I couldn't help realizing how dramatically the healing effects of God's love could be demonstrated if some teen-agers could leave Teen Challenge and go back to the slums where they would live among the same hopeless people, the same filth, and the same degradation, and yet remain untouched by it.

Now I suddenly realized that such a longing was as unrealistic as it was foolish. When some boys and girls came in off the streets and into the center, they were literally crawling out of a snake pit. Did I want to throw them back just to prove to some people on the sidelines that they were immune to snake bite?

I made a sharp left turn and slowly zig-zagged down a short street where I knew almost every surly boy who lounged in an open doorway or leaned against a car parked along the curb. It was a hot night and most of the boys wore limp, dark cotton slacks and shirts—the slacks tight and faded at the creases behind the knees and the unpressed shirts open down the front. How different they looked from the boys I had seen earlier in the day!

I made another left turn and worked my way back toward the center. It was really only a few blocks away from those kids, but whenever any of them tried to make the journey the streets fought him every step of the way.

# 2

I put the question to Billy that night as I fixed a snack in the kitchen.

"Do you think you would have made it, Billy? Could you have gone back to the old turf and stayed clean?"

"Not on your life!" Billy's answer came with a grunt as he stretched for a bag of doughnuts on the top shelf of the cupboard. "Don't forget, Davie, I wasn't on H then—but you can't live on those streets and stay out of the gangs. Not if you want to stay alive."

"Even if you came back with an education? Even if you came back as an ordained minister?" Although I had my ideas on the subject, Billy could speak with the authority of firsthand experience.

"Listen," Billy sat on a chair across from me and leaned intently across the table, "I can go out on those streets now—every day and every night, sometimes—and I can take a lot of abuse from guys who are just the way I used to be. It doesn't hurt me. I've got strength I never had a few years ago, and I know where it comes from. But I'm not trapped in that turf any more, Davie. I can come out of it after I go into it—and I can come here for a clean bed and a good meal. I pass a lot of guys in these halls and my hands don't have to reach for my knife." Abruptly he stopped and his round face broke into a grin. "You know what I reach for now, Davie?

My Bible! Almost every time I pass some kid in a hall or sit down at a table with him, he wants to ask me a question about something in the Bible!"

I laughed with him. "I guess that answers the last of my doubts, Billy. Hand me a doughnut, will you?"

He pushed the bag across the table. "Finish them off. You're getting so thin, the kids'll think you're a streetlight one of these days."

I took his advice and was busy chewing when Al Lorenzo poked his head into the kitchen. I waved him in and Billy poured him a glass of milk.

I hadn't seen Al for a long time and I missed his special touch at the center. He wasn't one of our regular workers, but whenever he dropped by to see how things were going, he always seemed to have the right word for a boy who needed it. He didn't live in our neighborhood, but some of his relatives did, and most of the gangs knew him at least by sight as someone who belonged. A familiar face was important to kids who considered an enemy to be anyone they didn't recognize.

Al was a heavy man and he sat in the chair carefully, as though he were accustomed to sitting on chairs that needed repairs. Ours were good and sturdy, and he relaxed. I thought I knew why he was in such a quiet mood. It had a lot to do with his unusual absence from the center.

"I haven't changed my mind, Al," I said, as gently as I could, for this gentle man was my good friend.

"It's worse, Dave, much worse."

"Did you tell your nephew what I said?"

"I told him—I told him." He put his hands flat on the table, palms down, and his fingers were very rigid. "You know what? He laughs at me!"

"That's not unusual, Al. We're used to horselaughs around here." And so we were. Those of us who went out to preach on street corners were greeted with worse than laughter much of the time. But it was harder on Al because he didn't go out every day trying to tell foul-mouthed boys and girls about God's love. Al was one of the kindest men I had ever known and he was suffering because he couldn't help his nephew.

Gregory Lorenzo, Al's nephew, was one of the boys I had seen on the street earlier that day. We had noticed him before Al came to us about him, but he wasn't the kind we could help. Gregory was in more trouble than I could list, but it hadn't yet scared him enough. That's why I had to say no when Al asked me to speak to Gregory and try to bring him to the center.

"Dave," he said, and he seemed to pit every ounce of his large body against the tears forming in his eyes, "I don't think you understand how bad he is."

I stood up and pushed the chair away from me. "Don't I? Then what makes him worse than the other boys I've seen every day for years?" Al looked at Billy in hurt surprise at my tone. "Does he steal?" I asked. "That's nothing new to me! Does he mug people for a buck? Does he smoke marijuana? Shoot heroin? Go ahead, Al, try to shock me! What's different about him?"

"Sure, Dave, he does those things, all right," Al said. "But now it's worse. These boys he hangs around with—they're real bad, Dave." He hung his head. "They're homosexuals! And Greg goes along with them because they pay him!"

How deeply Al was hurt! Both Billy and I could feel it and we reached out to touch his shoulder. It was such a futile gesture of comfort.

"Al," I said, and I thought carefully as I spoke, "I'll tell you again why I can't do anything for Greg. As low as he is in your eyes, he's got to fall farther—he's got to be lying flat on his back at the bottom of a black pit before he realizes he needs help. That's when we can help him—and that's why we insist that kids have to come here under their own steam."

Al lifted his strong hands and slammed them down on the table. "But you do go out and talk to some boys! You try to talk them into giving up their old ways!"

"Yes, Al, we do everything we can to persuade the ones we think we can reach." I sat down across from him. "Look, when we talk to a boy and tell him that God loves him and wants him to be happy, we can see whether we're getting through to him. Some pull away, even though they want to believe, and we go after them because they admit they're junkies or hoods and they don't like the way they have to live. But boys like Gregory—Al, he *likes* the way he lives!"

"You know what he's doing now, Dave? He's just like his father used to be. I followed him one night last week—he goes to a rathole of a place. It's supposed to be a condemned building, with nobody in it—but somebody's there, all right. A girl lives there and the kids go in for a fix."

"A shooting gallery," Billy interrupted.

"A what?"

"They call it a shooting gallery. It means the girl not only pushes narcotics but supplies the needles and all the other equipment—she sort of rents it out."

"You see how bad it is, Dave? And Greg could be a real good boy—he's not like those boys he runs around with."

There was only one thing we could do for Al's nephew at this point. "Come on, Al," I said and went toward the door.

"Maybe we can't get anywhere talking to Greg now—but we can talk to God." Billy came with us to the chapel.

I was still thinking about Al Lorenzo when my mother came into my office and put an armful of Bibles on my desk.

"These need repairs, David," she said briskly. "But I guess that's good. It means they're used."

I always enjoy talking to my mother, but she had no time for me that evening. "I'm meeting Fay down in the Village."

"Still preaching in the park?"

"I most certainly am! And we could use a young man like you down there any time you want to stop looking down your nose at us." That blunt answer and the twinkle in the light blue eyes were typical of my mother, who is a wonderful combination of a top sergeant and Mother Hubbard.

"Can you sit down for a minute?" I wanted to talk to her about a lot of things, but most of them were still too vague to put into words.

She seemed to sense my need. She sat in the armchair as though she had all the time in the world. "What's on your mind, David?"

I wasn't ready to go into my problems, and I hadn't given enough time to hers lately. "Are you and Fay really getting any results down in the Village?" I asked her very seriously.

"I feel we are—although I can't line up any converts to prove it."

"Are you sure you aren't wasting your time, Mother? I know you spend your days here, but we can use all the time you've got to give."

I felt a little silly when my mother smiled at me so indulgently. "David, you sound like an old minister talking to a very young one. Don't forget—I was ordained the same year you were!"

"I'm sorry," I said. "I guess I was speaking more like a son than a minister."

She saw that I was beating around the bush and, considerate though she is, she had important things to do. "That's all right—you are both. And I need your help in both ways." She wagged her finger at me. "You think these beatniks in Greenwich Village are a lot of phonies, don't you?"

"No, not really—"

"Well, they aren't, not any more than your young gang friends are! They're in trouble, deep trouble, and God is the only one who can do anything with them." She frowned. "If I could only find the way to tell them about Him."

"They're beginning to listen to you when you preach in the park, aren't they?"

"Yes, but that isn't enough. We need a place—"

I interrupted with a smile I couldn't control. "Like a center?" I asked.

"No, David, a center might not be the thing for the Village. Things are different there. Still, I need a place. . . ." Her voice trailed off and she glanced at her wristwatch. "Got to go. See you." And she was gone.

I stayed in my office until very late that night. Gwen and the children were away for the week, and the sounds of the center made me feel I was with a family, my family. In a way, every young boy or girl who came past that front door became a member of my family, because I loved each one of them.

Some people thought we were a noisy crowd, and sitting there that night I had to admit they were right. From the boys' dormitory down the hall came the sounds of a bull session, probably the most amazing one in the world. Leading the session and answering some of the toughest questions was Billy, who had led one of the most dangerous teen gangs in New York. Sitting on the bunk beds were boys who bore the scars of knives and needles on their bodies and the wounds of neglect in their souls. They had questions to ask, questions about God and the Bible, and they wanted straight answers.

Upstairs in the girls' dormitory Carmen was conducting the same kind of meeting, and now and then, as the debate got heated, I could hear their voices.

The door of the chapel opened and before it closed again I heard a girl praying: "O Lord, let Thy Spirit move upon my heart. . . ."

There must have been three or four kids in the kitchen having a late snack, and I was soothed by the clang of pots and the clatter of dishes. I remembered a time when there was rarely enough food for an extra meal at the center and sometimes we had to skip a regular one. Whenever the supplies got very low, we went into the chapel and thanked God for the food He was going to provide for us—and we never missed more than one meal. Sometimes a few young hoods laughed aloud when we "prayed the food in," but it didn't seem foolish to most of us. We knew that a God who could save our souls would certainly give us enough food to eat.

All these sounds were pretty boisterous and I loved having them around me while I worked. They were the steady sounds of joy, not the nervous shouts of fear.

Later, when the building was quiet, I found I couldn't

work as well. I don't like paperwork anyway, and I couldn't eliminate the large mound that lay on my desk. Strange, but I never used to have much paperwork a few years ago.

I was restless and got up to stand by a window. It was cooler there, I told myself, but that wasn't my reason. I was beginning to feel as if I were on the outside, looking in, and I didn't like it.

Before we got the center my problems were simple—gigantic but simple. I had to look for kids in trouble with the law, kids on narcotics, kids in the gangs, thieves, addicts, prostitutes, muggers, killers—and tell them about the God who loved them. I had to wait until they stopped being afraid of me, until they began to trust me, until they began to believe what I said. I had to find a haven for them. Sometimes I had some practical problems of my own—a place to stay, food to eat, getting my family settled in the city—but they never seemed overwhelming.

Teen Challenge had grown very fast in a few short years. Were we growing too fast? Were our files and correspondence crowding the Holy Spirit out of the organization? I found myself wondering about these things much more often lately, especially when I didn't get to the center as often as I wanted.

I looked out on the dark, quiet street. The streetlight gleamed beyond the neat iron fence that separated our green front lawn from the sidewalk, and I tried to see beyond the light into the dark wall of life. There were kids out there, even though I couldn't see them, and I wanted to be out looking for them. I should have been doing that tonight instead of working at a desk.

# 3

I got back to the center two days later and found my desk top almost cleared. One look at the overflowing wastebasket told me that my mother had declared war on my paperwork.

I no sooner sat down than the telephone rang.

"Reverend Wilkerson, maybe you can help me out." It was a prison social worker who had become interested in Teen Challenge. She worked at the Women's House of Detention and had sent several released prisoners in our direction.

"It's usually the other way around," I said. "Glad to return the favor."

"Well—" she paused and seemed at a loss for words. "I know this may sound crazy, but here goes. There's a girl here named Molly Stevens. She gets out today and I've been trying to talk her into going to Teen Challenge. Up until today I couldn't get anywhere with her." She paused again and I heard her take a deep breath. "Reverend Wilkerson, this girl tells me that she put out a fleece a few days ago—does that make any sense to you?"

Now I was the puzzled one. "Yes—and no. Is there more to the story?"

"Yes. Now she wants to go to the center—but there's a hitch to it."

"Why?"

"Molly's not a teen-ager. She's thirty years old. Now, does that conflict with Teen Challenge?"

"Oh, don't worry about that," I said. "We take people past their teens if they really want help. Is she an addict?"

"For fifteen years."

"How did she ever live this long? Not many of them do."

"You should have seen her when she came here a year ago. She was sent up for pushing heroin, and she looked half dead." Her voice trailed off and I heard only silence. When she spoke again, she covered her emotions with the clipped tones of efficiency. "Well—she wants you to meet her when she gets out at 10:30 this morning. Can you do it—or send somebody from the center?"

"You know I can."

"You know better than to get your hopes up, too. One step outside the door and these gals want only one thing—a fix."

The Women's House of Detention is one of the most forbidding buildings I have ever seen. I first saw it one night a few years ago when I was driving through Greenwich Village with Paul DiLena, a Transit Authority Police captain and good friend of Teen Challenge. We had just passed a tall building—in the darkness I could only see its silhouette rising above some smaller buildings—but there was something very depressing about it.

"What's that place?" I asked Paul.

He shook his head grimly. "The polite name for it is *The Women's House of Detention.* If you want to be more accurate, you might call it *Hell.*"

I kept looking at it in the rearview mirror after we passed. I could see lots of lights shining out of the barred, unshaded windows, but the lights didn't twinkle as they did in most New York buildings. They just glared out into the night.

Eventually I came to know the building quite well. It was a jail for women. The ages of the prisoners ranged from girlhood to old age, and their crimes included everything from breaking into a basement to murder. No distinctions were made among the prisoners, and if a girl went in to serve a sentence for petty burglary she could come out well trained in the fine points of the narcotics trade.

Jail is a sickening experience, even for the most hardened hoodlums, and I could understand why most prisoners made desperate vows to reform once they got out. It wasn't that they craved a better life for its own sake—they just didn't want to go back to the horrors of jail again. But the old way of life was always waiting for them outside the door, and very few ever escaped its grasp.

Still, whenever we got a call from anybody in jail we always answered it.

I took Joe Catessi and Hope Soto, two of our best Teen Challenge workers, with me to meet Molly. We met her in the reception room inside the front door. It was a cold, dingy room that seemed to tell the despairing people who came and went that they would find no sympathy there. That day the room was crowded.

I didn't expect a young girl, but when I saw Molly I wondered whether she had ever looked young. She had been off narcotics during the year she spent in the House of Detention, so her eyes weren't glazed over, but there was a terrible deadness in them.

There was nothing dead about the rest of her. She made

an incredible number of jarring little noises as she came toward us. She was chewing gum, clacking it loudly in her teeth, and her scuffed, high-heeled shoes scraped along the floor in an uneven rhythm. The most disturbing noises came from her jewelry. Her arms were tinny jangles of bracelets that slid up and down, crashing into each other every time she reached up to flatten a straggly mouse-colored curl of hair against a thin, sallow cheek. Hanging from her ear lobes were large gold-colored hoops fastened to smaller loops that hung from holes pierced in her ears. She moved her head constantly in quick, jerking turns from one side to the other, and the earrings never stayed still. As they moved they made an irritating, leaden, whirring sound which apparently was pleasing to her.

Even Molly's clothes were noisy. Her skirt, ridiculously short and tight, was bright red, and her sleazy, clinging blouse was striped in electric shades of blue and green.

The matron who brought her out to us knew us and made a few brief introductions. As she left Molly sneered after her. Then she put her hands on her hips and planted her thin, bony legs as far apart as her meager skirt would allow and looked us over suspiciously. I put out my hand, and after she had studied it carefully, she shook it briefly. Pointing to Hope and Joe, she said, "They been hooked?"

"No," Joe answered, patiently.

"I thought you had ex-junkies working with you!" she said, turning to me accusingly.

"I do—some of them, anyway. Joe and Hope are Bible students working at Teen Challenge Center now." As I talked she craned her long, thin neck to look past us and all around the room. Already she was forgetting the degrading cell that had been her home for the past year.

It was important to hold her attention. "What about this fleece business, Molly?" I asked.

She jerked her head around to me and shifted her weight to another foot, jangling her jewelry as she moved. "You don't believe it, do you? I'm not good enough to put out a fleece?"

"Look, don't put on the sympathy act—I won't fall for it!" She was trying to stall, and she would weaken with every moment she eked out.

"All right, all right!" she grumbled. "I read your book—the one about the switchblade."

"*The Cross and the Switchblade,*" Hope corrected gently, leaning heavily on the first part of the title.

Molly ignored her. "I guess you thought I couldn't read. Well, I'm not like the rest of these junkies—I been through eighth grade."

"How did you get the book, Molly?" I asked.

"They loaned it to me upstairs." She was referring to the prison library. "The cover looks good, so I says, okay, I'll give it a try. But it's a real dud at first."

"Why?"

"Who wants to read about God? He don't ever come here on visiting days."

"Yes, He does, Molly. He's here all the time."

Her eyes narrowed, only briefly. Then she let her hands drop loosely at her side and the bracelets collided at her wrists. "I read it, all the way through," she said, as though she were ashamed.

"What about the fleece, Molly," I persisted.

She had lost interest in the front door and any other part of the room. At last she was silent, motionless. "I got to the part about that guy, Gideon. He thought God wanted him to do something, but he wasn't sure he got the message straight. So he put out a fleece—on the ground overnight—and he asks God to let the fleece stay dry if He really wants Gideon to do this thing." Molly's dark eyes widened as she spoke. "You know, Rev'rn, I had to ask a matron what a fleece was—and she had to ask somebody else. Then she told me it was a piece of wool.

"There was this other woman—I think she's a social worker—who kept telling me I should call Teen Challenge and see if I could go there when I got out. But—I don't know—I felt kinda funny. I'm not a kid—I'm over twenty-one, anyway."

Hope reached for Molly's hand. "You wanted something better in life, didn't you, Molly?"

"Sure! It's got to get better! I've been through all the rotten things in life. I don't want to go back! But it ain't easy—not after so many years!"

"You've been in jail before—did you feel different about it this time?" I asked.

She was defensive again. Her mouth turned down in a sneer and she threw her head back arrogantly. "This time I got a message," she said, pausing for emphasis. "I had a feeling that God wanted me to straighten myself out—but I wasn't so sure I could trust that feeling.

"Look, Rev'rn, I ain't never seen dew—I hardly ever seen grass—but I thought I'd try this fleece business, like I read in your book."

"I read about it in another Book, Molly," I interrupted, taking my Bible out of my pocket. I put it in her hands and closed her fingers around it. "You'll find Gideon in here, and a lot of other people—even yourself."

She was hesitant, but no longer suspicious, and as she

stared at me I realized that she had the emptiest eyes I had ever seen. I couldn't even see my own reflection in them. Then, as I watched, I saw a flicker of light in her eyes—but it was a light I recognized all too well. Molly was looking past me at something behind me. Without turning around I knew who it was—he didn't need a name or a face; he was a pusher and I recognized him by that weird light of longing in an addict's eyes.

"Tell you what," Molly said in a light breezy tone, "I'll come over to the center tonight. I gotta go see my family first." She handed the Bible back to me.

"You don't have a family, Molly," I said. I knew we would have to fight for her, and the odds, as usual, were against us. Joe and Hope realized it, too, and none of us dared take our eyes off Molly for a second—sometimes a soul can get lost in less time than that.

"Tell us about your fleece, Molly," I said, trying to keep her attention. "What did you use in place of a fleece?"

"Nothin'," she answered, and her voice began to rise nervously. "I don't have nothin' anyway. I just asked God to make it rain." She reached out and touched my hand; it was a pathetic gesture of charity from a woman who had never known any. "Trust me," she said, but the jangling of her bracelets and earrings beat time to her agitation. "I'll come tonight—honest!"

I pulled my hand away and seized her wrist. "Trust an addict? I know better than that, Molly! You're trying to chicken out on us! You were scared stiff when you were in jail, so you thought you'd try to bribe God with a lot of fancy promises!"

"No!" she whispered. She was afraid to start a scene. "I want to straighten out! Do you think I want to die in the gutter? I did pretty good in jail—I been off the stuff for a whole year!"

"And that's not enough, is it? I think you know you can't lick this problem by yourself." Again she looked anxiously over my shoulder, and I knew the pusher was still there. "Tell me about the rain, Molly! Don't look over there at him! Why did you want the rain?"

It was a physical struggle for her to turn her head and look at me. "I didn't really want to believe that feeling I had. I knew what it would mean—goin' to that center with a lot of kids and all. I wanted a fix so bad—I didn't want to make up my mind to stay off it." The eerie light in her eyes was beginning to fade. "I don't pray good, but I said, 'Lord, if You're really there, and if You really want me to go out of here and learn how to live a good life—then You gotta help me, startin' right now. Lord,' I said, 'if that's what You want, let it rain real hard tomorrow. Let it pour!' "

"And did it rain?"

"Did it? You remember last Wednesday? That day it came down in buckets?"

"Yes, Molly, it really poured."

Molly seemed to slump with exhaustion—the pusher was gone. "I didn't want it to rain that morning—I didn't want to get up and look out the window. But I could hear it beatin' on the wall outside." She smiled weakly. "I didn't want you to come today, either, but you came. I guess I'm real chicken."

"No, Molly," I said. "I know what you just went through. That took guts." Hope took her arm as we turned and went to the door.

"This I gotta have," Molly said stubbornly, jamming a cigarette in her mouth as we pulled up in front of the center.

"I'm sorry, Molly—" Hope began.

"Oh, no! You gotta leave me somethin'."

Hope looked at me with a plea for support in her large, sympathetic eyes.

"Get rid of them—now!" I said. "They're only a crutch and you've got to learn to walk on your own two feet."

"Suppose I fall flat on my face!"

"Then get up again!"

Angrily she pulled the cigarette from her mouth and threw it on the sidewalk. She tugged at the enormous, shiny, black bag slung over her shoulder and dug deep down in it. Then she took out a wrinkled, half-empty pack of cigarettes and threw it down, grinding it under her pointed shoes. All the time her eyes bored into mine and I knew that she could have ground me into the sidewalk, too.

Hope took her upstairs and I followed a few minutes later. When Molly saw the sunny, chintz-curtained room that was to be her temporary home, she sank down on the bed and shook her head slowly from side to side. The earrings whirred their leaden song.

"You should see some of the places I slept in," she said, closing her eyes in disgust at the memory of them. "You get so you'll do anything for a fix—I guess I been in the worst dumps in town. Sometimes I couldn't remember goin' to them—sometimes I didn't even remember who took me there."

I wondered whether tears would fall from those tragically dull eyes. Molly's apology for life held such a lonely longing that I felt my own eyes misting over, but hers were dry. It made the pain in her soul seem even more agonizing.

Al Lorenzo had promised to come for supper that night, but he didn't show up. That wasn't unusual—he had a lot of relatives and a great big heart that went out to them all. He'd come when he could. But later, when Al called from a precinct station, a friendly supper was the last thing on his mind.

Gregory Lorenzo had been arrested in a raid on the shooting gallery. Actually, the police didn't find anything resembling a big narcotics ring; they found a few bedraggled kids deep in the stupor of drugs, a morbid collection of hypodermics, syringes, bottle-cap cookers, and little packets of innocent-looking powder that carried a high price tag—the body, mind, and soul of anyone who got to like it.

Rose Martinez, the girl who ran the shooting gallery, apparently had some influence in important places and she was released soon after her arrest. The others—Greg and his hopped-up companions—were kept in jail.

I knew what Al was going to ask me before he said it, but again I had to refuse to see his nephew—unless, of course, the boy wanted to see me, which he didn't.

I felt so useless. Al was a good friend who would have given his life for me—and there didn't seem to be anything I could do for him. I was failing him—I knew it. Was I failing God, too?

Billy didn't approve of my reaction to Al's call and he let me know it. "Sure, I know all about the rules, Dave," he said. "I live by them, too. But this kid ought to be an exception."

I was disappointed that Billy, of all people, was willing to overlook the fact that nothing could help these kids unless they wanted help. Wasn't he one of the worst holdouts a few years ago when I began to preach in the slums? Had he forgotten what he did when I first held out my hand to him?

He spat on my shoes and actually cursed me! It took a long time for Billy to surrender his life to God and I wasn't the one who brought him around to it—the Spirit did that, and in His own time. Sure, I told Billy about God's love for him, many times, but I wasn't the one who opened his heart to it and brought him to his knees right in front of his own gang members.

I didn't want to let Billy see my annoyance, so I cut short our discussion of Gregory Lorenzo. I went down the hall to look in on another boy, Mario, who had resisted help down to the last minute—but in that last minute he had come to our front door.

Mario had barged into the center the previous night, while I was away, but Joe had told me about him and asked me to look in on him.

His first twenty-four hours at the center had been rough, but he was beginning to show signs of recovery. Although it didn't happen often, I had seen some people experience a relatively easy withdrawal, and Mario appeared to be one of them.

He was sitting up in bed when I came in. Joe sat on a folding chair beside the bed, reading aloud from the Bible. Neither of them looked up when I came in and I stood by the door, reluctant to interrupt. Something about the atmosphere in that room was so peaceful and reassuring that I felt my own tensions begin to relax.

Mario's face was quite pale, but at least it wasn't a sickly green, as Joe had said it was when he came in. He was waving a long, ugly knife then and threatening to kill his wife and himself. He couldn't stand the things he did to buy the heroin he craved. When a boy is on a $45-a-day habit he can't supply his needs with a regular job—he has to steal the money from people and sometimes he has to hurt them to get it.

Mario's wife wouldn't leave him, so he tried to leave her because he couldn't look at the pain in her eyes when she forgave him time after time. But it didn't work out—he kept coming back to his wife, but only to steal whatever he could find in her purse.

Several times he had managed to break the habit—for a few days, anyway—but he couldn't stay clean. Once he stayed off narcotics long enough to pass the physical exam for the merchant marine and he thought his problems were solved when he was accepted as a seaman. Maybe if he could go all over the world that would be better than getting high on a fix.

Mario went all over the world, all right, and he ran into pushers in every port. If anything, heroin was easier to come by, and eventually he became such an incompetent seaman that he had to leave the merchant marine.

When he got back to Brooklyn he began to live according to a regular and terrifying pattern—a pusher, a jail cell, and a phone call to his wife! He could think of only one way to end it.

"Hey, Dave," Joe called, realizing I was standing behind him. He introduced me to Mario and I pulled up another chair while Joe continued to read. When he finished, he looked up at the boy on the bed. "Do you dig this, Mario?"

Mario had small round brown eyes and at that moment they looked slightly sheepish. "No—I'm not used to that kind of talk. But that's okay, don't get me wrong! I like it—it sounds good even though I don't understand it."

"That's good enough—for now, at least," Joe said. "You'll get the hang of the language after a while, but I think you're getting the message already."

Mario laughed in embarrassment. "It's funny," he said to me as Joe left, "but I got a lot of help from that Book. All last night, all day today, somebody was in here reading it to me. They took turns. Sometimes I was rolling all over the bed, trying to bang my head against the wall, so I didn't think I even heard what they were saying—but I did. This morning, when I woke up, I knew it wasn't going to be like those other times. I felt so much better after just one day."

"Mario, if we could go through your suffering for you, we'd gladly do it," I said.

Mario drew up his knees and clasped his arms around them. "I called my wife tonight—she thought I was calling from jail again. When she heard where I was, she cried—she couldn't talk, she just cried. Then I cried, too—what a mess!"

"You were in pretty bad shape last night," I reminded him. "I hear you wanted to kill yourself—your wife, too."

He shook his head and ran his fingers nervously through his shiny black hair. "I had it. I couldn't take it no more. Those things I did—don't get me wrong, I've never been an angel—but I was just dirt."

"Did your wife tell you about the center?"

"Yeah—she heard about it from a friend of hers. But I wanted no part of it. I thought it was just another phony cure—I didn't want to go pray with a bunch of holy joes!"

"But you didn't want to die, either, did you?" He looked at me angrily. "That's right, Mario, and I thank God you wanted to live. Isn't that why you came here? Weren't we the last chance you had?"

The anger slowly left his eyes. He tightened his arms around his legs and rested his cheek on his knees. "I still don't know if I can buy this stuff about God loving me. If He loved me, why did He let me get hooked?"

"That was your own doing, Mario—and a lot of evil things in the world helped you along the way. You can't expect God to reach out and slap your wrist every time you do something you know is wrong."

I stood and went to the foot of the bed where I could get a look at his face. "Look, Mario, last night you were going to take your life, right?" He nodded. "Well, that's not the answer. You've got to *give* your life—give it to God and let Him make something good out of it." He frowned. "If you won't give your life to Him, then you'll go on calling the signals, and you know what that means!" Mario's face was screwed up in such furrows of concentration that I thought he might be making fun of me. He wasn't. The yawn that stretched his mouth and smoothed his forehead was genuine —he was exhausted from shifting through the debris of his life, and he sank back upon the bed.

"Get some sleep, Mario," I said, softly, pulling the blankets up around his chin. "God will still be waiting for you tomorrow." He was asleep before I closed the door. Joe was waiting in the hall and he went back to sit by a boy who might awaken during the night and need to know that a friend was near.

Mario had helped me, too. Before I talked to him I had begun to wonder whether I was doing the right thing for Gregory. I knew now that I was. I was following God's will for his life.

"O Lord," I prayed that night in the chapel, "forgive me for questioning Your way. Did I really think I could work among these tormented young people without feeling some of their pain? When I have to stand by and watch one of them destroying himself—refusing the love that could save him, let me remember that You also watch, and weep, and bear his pain—only many more times than I could ever endure."

I wept as I prayed. I wept for Al Lorenzo, for Greg, and for all the lost young lives. And I wept for God.

# 4

Some amazing things happened to Molly during her first week at the center.

I noticed the change in her appearance as soon as I saw her again. I had been away for several days on a trip to so many cities that I was dizzy at the thought of them—Chicago, Detroit, St. Louis, Los Angeles, San Francisco.

As soon as I rested up at home I went to the center and ran right into Molly.

"Hi, Brother Dave!" she said, and her big smile became a laugh of delight when she saw that I didn't recognize her immediately.

"Molly?" I said.

"The old bag herself!" she said proudly.

"Well, you look about fifty years younger!" It was not an exaggeration. Her eyes no longer retreated from the light of day and they sparkled with reflections. She wasn't wearing any makeup but her face glowed with color and her cheeks were filling out. The biggest improvement was the absence of the absurd distracting earrings. Then I noticed how quiet Molly was—she had given up the bracelets, too.

She seemed to read my thoughts. "Yeah, I know what you mean," she said, holding up her arms and shaking her hands in a caricature of herself. "No more jingle-jangle, either."

"How come?"

"They looked stupid!"

"But you didn't think so last week."

Molly bit her lip. "Last week those loops were all I had. They made me feel important.

"You are important, Molly. You're important to God."

Her smile returned. "I thought everybody was nuts when they kept telling me that. Then I thought, 'Look, did you ever get so much attention in your whole life? If these people can care about you, maybe all they say about God is true.' So, I looked in the mirror one day and I saw a jerk! I thought, 'If you want to find out how much God loves you, at least meet Him halfway!' So, off came the bangles."

I had to smile, as I often do, when I hear someone like Molly describe her growing awareness of God. This girl had been on very familiar terms with hell during her life, but God had seemed a stranger to her, nothing more than a name she used to hear at Christmas and Easter. Now she was reaching out to find God, and when she did she would grasp His hand with both of hers and never let go.

The Mollys in this world don't worry about grammar and phrasing when they pray. They don't even care where they are when they want to talk to God. He is very real to them; He isn't a remote supervisor of their lives—He is the most vital part of their existence.

Molly had only begun to realize what love could do for her. She had a long way to go, and she would often be tempted to drop out along the way, but she would have Someone strong to turn to whenever she felt weak.

I thought Molly was coming along well enough to go up to the Teen Challenge home for girls in Rhinebeck, New York. The spacious former mansion did for girls what the farm did for boys. There they had a chance to be healed in body, mind, and soul.

After notifying our superintendent, Rev. Allen Mitchell, that I would bring Molly up the next day, I wondered whether Mario was ready to go to the farm. But I hadn't caught up with the latest news—Mario couldn't wait to go and Joe Catessi was going to drive him there in the afternoon.

"But somethin's buggin' me," he said when I called him into my office to say goodbye. I pointed to a chair and he sat on the edge of it. "I think I oughta make good for some of the things I've done—they're startin' to bother me."

Whenever a boy or girl is able to stick it out with Teen Challenge, he usually comes to this point in his life. Mario was coming to it a little earlier than most.

Restitution is a necessary part of our rehabilitation program and we certainly encouraged our converts to do it, wherever possible. But most of them have done such terrible, senseless things in their past that specific restitution is either impossible or unthinkable. Very often their acts of violence are parts of a pattern of vengeance that is hopelessly tangled. And in too many instances their fury has been aimed at strangers whose names were never known.

It is easy to understand why these kids want to repair with love what they have demolished with hate, but it is something to be undertaken after much thought and deep prayer.

"I sent some people to the hospital—maybe some even died," Mario said. "I'd pick out a guy on his way home—I didn't even know him—and clobber him from behind. Once I waited around for a long time when one guy didn't start to come to. He just didn't move! Then I heard someone comin' and I ran. When I went back later, nobody was around, but there was blood on the sidewalk." Tears fell from his eyes. "I only got a couple of dollars from him—not even enough for a fix," he said bitterly.

"Mario, what can you do for that man now?" I asked him.

"How should I know?" he said, and he stood up impatiently. "Maybe I could turn myself in—maybe I could pay his hospital bills if he's still alive!"

"But you don't even know his name or where he lives!"

"The cops could find out—they could!"

He was so repelled by his crimes that he would have assumed the blame for one he didn't commit. I couldn't let him go to the farm with such a weight of guilt on his mind.

I picked up the telephone and motioned Mario to sit down again. "We'll find out as much as we can about that man." I called Paul DiLena and explained Mario's circumstances. He understood immediately—it wasn't the first time he had investigated the consequences of violence for us.

I told Mario not to worry. I knew Paul wanted to help any kids break free of a life of crime but he wouldn't let them make a mockery of the law.

While we waited for word from Paul I told Mario about the time Sonny had wanted to go to the police about an old burglary charge against him. The crime went back to the days before he came to Teen Challenge and he had made matters worse by jumping bail. A lawyer advised us that unless Sonny pleaded innocent he would surely end up with some kind of jail sentence, whichever way the verdict went, but Sonny would have no part of it. He had learned the meaning of the truth from Jesus and he would never compromise it again.

Paul DiLena came with Sonny and me to court on the day the case was to be heard. Paul had never appeared in court in behalf of any of the boys who came to the center, but the thought of Sonny being sent to jail when he was beginning to find spiritual freedom was too much for him.

The sight of that tall, heavy, intelligent-looking man taking his place beside the slim, frightened boy who still bore the physical scars of addiction made me swallow hard. I wondered whether a judge, who must hear moving pleas every day of his life, could possibly look on them without emotion.

When Paul stood up and spoke, I never would have known that he was a stranger in court. His voice was clear and he didn't waste a word. The lawyer appointed to Sonny's case almost threw up his hands in despair when Paul immediately stated Sonny's plea of guilt and then began to tell the judge about the boy's life at the time he committed the burglary.

"I'm not asking you to overlook his crime because he had a rough time in life—which he did. But I couldn't plead for mercy on that basis because I know such a boy would go right back to the same kind of life." Paul paused and took a deep breath. I felt my hands getting moist and while part of me listened intently to every word Paul said, the rest of me began to pray to God.

"Your Honor," Paul said, "I ask for mercy in the full knowledge that this boy has left that way of life far behind him. This is not a promise or a lot of empty words. I've seen what his new life, in the power of the Spirit, has made of him. I've seen him go out on the streets with a Bible in his hand. I've seen him walk up to a hostile gang of boys and tell them how much Jesus loves them and wants to help them. I've seen him stand calm and unafraid when they threaten him with fists or knives—he didn't raise a hand when one of them pushed him to the ground. He looked up at the boy—a vicious little punk—and said, 'You don't wan't to hurt me. I wouldn't do anything to harm you. I love you!'"

I cleared my throat and it sounded like thunder in the stillness of the room.

Paul put his hand on Sonny's shoulder. "Your Honor, God has given this boy a new life. I ask you to give him a chance to live it in the service of God. This is also a practical plea, Your Honor, because Sonny may save some boys who might otherwise come to stand here in this same court."

I could hear a lot of sniffling then and some people held handkerchiefs up to their faces. The judge sat quite still, his head bent thoughtfully. Then he looked up and spoke directly to Sonny.

"Young man," he said sternly, "there's always the chance that you're a phony. But these people who vouch for you certainly aren't. I'm going to sentence you, because according to law I must in this case—but I'm going to suspend sentence."

A lot of people must have been holding their breath along with me because they suddenly gave a long sigh of relief all at once.

The judge held up his hand for silence. He turned again to Sonny. "And, if you ever show up in this court again I'll throw the book at you!"

Sonny's story made sense to Mario, but he still jumped a little when the phone rang. It was Paul.

There was no police record of a mugging at the time and

place that Mario had described, and although Mario was known to the police as a young hood, their evidence against him had never been sufficient for an arrest. Legally he was in the clear, but his mind did not look upon his past with the cut and dry efficiency of the law.

"I wish I could find all those people so I could do something for them," he said, shaking his head.

"You can't, Mario," I said, "but there's another way you can make up for the harm you've done."

His eyes brightened eagerly. "Anything! Honest, I'll do anything!"

"Do what Sonny and Billy and a lot of others are doing now. Go out and try to help some other kid who might be heading in the same direction you took—try to help a boy before he becomes a mugger or a murderer. If you do that, you can help a lot of people you'll never even see. They'll never be able to thank you for it or tell you what a wonderful guy you are—if praise is what you want. You won't find a welcome mat out there on the streets, either! You go out there with a Bible in your hand and you'll see how rough it is!"

Mario pressed his hands to his temples and closed his eyes. I could have said more, but I didn't know how much he was ready to take. We asked something similar of a lot of the kids who came to the center and many of them had to drop out before they really understood what we were trying to say.

When Mario dropped his hands and sat forward, I wondered whether he was going to be one more boy who walked out the door because he had expected us to use some kind of magic formula to transform him instantaneously.

"When do I start?" he said, with that disarmingly sheepish smile.

"Right now. We've got a lot to talk about!" I said, reaching for my Bible. I wasn't the least bit tired any more.

It had been a strenuous day and before I went home for dinner I sat at my desk trying to sort out the thoughts in my mind.

I was still uneasy about the way I used my time. I never seemed to spend enough hours in one place and my itinerary kept getting more complicated.

In every town I had visited during the previous week I was met with questions, and more questions, about Teen Challenge. During the past year I had helped set up some much-needed centers in Los Angeles, San Francisco, Chicago, Philadelphia, Boston, and even Toronto, but many more were needed. Sometimes it broke my heart to speak to groups of people who were deeply disturbed about the crime and degradation that was snuffing out the futures and lives of many teen-agers. These people wanted to do something—and in their desperation they did almost anything—and paid any price. They set up expensive youth programs, hired social workers and recreation directors and psychiatrists to guide their lost young people. It seemed so strange to me that even among church groups, God was often the last resort.

Because more and more people wanted to hear about the Teen Challenge program, somebody had to go out and talk to them. I was that somebody—at least at the moment—but as soon as I could begin to share the job with somebody else,

I planned to spend more of my time in the center and out on the streets.

"Maybe then I'll feel at home again," I said to my mother. I had started to talk to her about her work in the Village, and here I was, talking about my problems.

"That may not be the answer, David," she said. "Perhaps you'll have to learn how to feel at home in many different places."

"Enough about me, now. I really want to know how things are going with you."

She sat very straight in the chair, with her clasped hands in her lap. "David, I was right—a center isn't quite what we need down there. I'm beginning to think we should plan to open a chapel."

"In the Village!"

"Save your biggest gasp for this—I don't mean an ordinary chapel. I want it to have tables and chairs, and we ought to serve coffee and doughnuts."

My mother has a good healthy sense of humor, but I knew she was absolutely serious at that moment. Still, I couldn't resist saying the remark that came to my mind. "*Free* coffee and doughnuts, of course—and a Bible on every table!"

I certainly didn't expect the response I got. She grinned delightedly and reached over to squeeze my arm. "David! I told you we needed your help! Yes, the coffee and doughnuts should be free—those beatniks don't have much money! And the Bibles! That's a wonderful idea!"

"I wasn't serious, Mother!" Disappointment clouded her face and the crinkled laughter lines at the corners of her blue eyes began to smooth out. "No, we can't afford to run a hangout for bums! Our costs are going up every day—we need every penny we get and we have to be sure we spend it where it will do some good!"

"David, do you think God stays out of the Village?" She stood up and pointed an angry finger at me. "You're becoming a spiritual snob!"

"Certainly God is in the Village—but nobody down there will ever admit it. Nothing is real there—even the phonies are phony!"

"Then they need twice as much healing!"

We weren't getting anywhere and I wanted to end our disagreement. "I'll make a deal with you. If you'll bring a convert—just *one* convert—from the Village, I'll give you all the help I can. We'll open that chapel, somehow!"

My mother is a small woman but when she draws herself up in triumph, as she did then, I always feel as though she towers over me. She put out her hand and I shook it resolutely. "It's a deal!" she said.

# 5

I was sorry to see it rain the next day. I was driving Molly up to our school for girls at Rhinebeck and I had looked forward to seeing the expression on her face when she got out into the countryside for the first time.

As it turned out, I wasn't disappointed. The rain made no difference to Molly—she had never known how far the human eye could see when a dirty building wasn't standing in its way.

The hills along the New York Thruway are worn down closer to the earth and aren't quite as green as the Pennsylvania hills, but they are still very beautiful. And on that day their summer colors were more vivid against the dark gray sky. When we began to drive into apple country Molly gasped at the sight of the trees with their ruddy burden. She knew, of course, that apples grow on trees, but she had only seen them in store windows, lined up in neat rows.

She leaned back in her seat and turned her head so that she could gaze out the window and rest her neck at the same time.

"So, this school is really a mansion, right?" she asked.

"Well, it was, before we bought it."

Molly rolled her head in my direction. "But it was a *real* mansion, wasn't it?" That was a very important detail to her.

"Yes, Molly," I chuckled, and for the umpteenth time I told her about the spacious, lovely house and its 100 acres of grounds that used to be part of the Astor estate.

Molly's curiosity wasn't unusual. Almost every girl who went to our school was fascinated with the prospect of living in a mansion—and that was something I could understand. Sometimes, when I looked back upon the obscure beginnings of Teen Challenge only a few years back, it was hard to believe that our growth wasn't a dream.

But everything about it was very real, including the miraculous way God had been leading us from step to step. Long before I ever knew we would need a home and a school for girls, God had led me to a man who would make it possible for us to get it. W. Clement Stone, chairman of the Combined Insurance Companies of America, took an early interest in the Teen Challenge program, and when we saw that our girls as well as our boys needed a place where they could study and contemplate the wonderful new life that lay before them, we were given a grant by the W. Clement Stone Foundation. It enabled us to buy the great stone mansion overlooking the regal upper Hudson River. Now we could offer the view to as many as seventy-five young women who had seen only the squalid horizons of street fighting, narcotics addiction, prostitution, and children conceived—and not always allowed to live—out of wedlock.

As we drove between the stone pillars at the entrance to the long winding driveway, Molly sat up suddenly and touched my arm lightly. "Could you pull over for a minute?" she asked.

I wasn't surprised, and I stopped the car under one of the trees lining the drive. I waited for her to speak.

Poor Molly. She hadn't mentioned her reluctance about living among teen-agers since the day we had met at the jail, but I knew it still bothered her. And she had come to an uncertain point between the misery she had known and the joy she hoped to find. Molly had given up her brassy ornaments but she still held on tightly to her life. She wasn't yet ready to surrender it completely and unconditionally to God—or anyone else. It was a bad life but it was all she knew—and she was terrified to step onto alien turf.

"I don't think I can stay here," she muttered.

"I can't make you stay, Molly," I said. "You're the one who has to do that." I didn't realize how much my disappointment showed in my eyes until I saw that hers were very moist. "Molly, you're crying!"

Molly blinked in amazement. She rubbed a hand across her eyes and stared at her wet knuckles. Then she forced herself to grin. "I oughta be cryin' for myself—not for you," she grumbled. "If you could see how sad you look, you'd cry, too."

I gave her my handkerchief and she tried to make fun of her need for it by blowing her nose very loudly. Finally her bony shoulders heaved with a deep sigh. "Am I gonna make it?" she asked, and it was more of a plea for help than a question.

I smiled. "Yes, Molly."

"I don't know. I look different, but I'm not really different—inside, I mean. I fight with people all the time—they don't like me, I guess." She tossed her head defiantly. "I can't blame them."

"That will change, too—but give it time."

"Is that what you teach at this school?" she asked, and I couldn't miss the sarcasm in her voice.

"If you want a lot of pat answers, you won't get them here," I said. I had had enough of her stalling and I started the motor again. I gave her enough time to get out in case she didn't want to go along.

She stayed and I pulled the car back onto the driveway.

A reception committee was waiting for us as we pulled up in front of the house, but Molly saw only the elegance of the building.

"Look at the chimneys!" she said. "You must light fires all over the place!"

Allen Mitchell offered his hand in a warm greeting but Molly brushed it lightly with her palm as she peered into the hall behind the open front door. She didn't even seem to notice Susan.

I had asked Allen to introduce Susan to Molly as soon as possible, but I knew I was taking a gamble by trying to encourage a friendship between the two girls. Susan was twenty-six and closer to Molly's age than any of the other girls at the school. But the two of them couldn't have been farther apart in temperament and background. Molly was a scrapper and Susan had gone down for the count a long time ago.

I thought we'd never get Molly past the entrance hall. The magnificent staircase, the high expanse of ceiling, and the warmth of the age-mellowed woodwork were designed to impress men who thought they were giants. To a girl like Molly, who was afraid she would live and die unnoticed, they were almost shattering.

I had a chance to watch Susan while we went on a tour of the first floor. She had come a long way since leaving the center, much further than I had dared to hope. Her tilted nose was no longer betrayed by a look of sadness in her delicate face. Now there was a vibrancy in her eyes.

The two girls had their first clash when we started up the stairs. Each step was wide and deep and Molly's tight skirt forced her to take them one at a time. Susan swept gracefully past her and smiled indulgently. "You'll have to let those seams out a bit, Molly," she said, "or else use the bannister."

Molly looked up in anger. "Somebody oughta tighten your lip!" she snapped and her free hand curled into a fist.

I expected Susan to turn and run, but she surprised me by stopping and offering Molly her hand. The warmth and friendship in her smile were unmistakable. "I wasn't trying to hurt your feelings," she said. "I just wanted you to be comfortable, Molly—I'm not very good at making people laugh, but I'm trying to learn."

Molly ignored the outstretched hand, but her fist uncurled.

Allen agreed that Susan's progress was exceptional. "She was one woebegone gal when she came up here," he said. "I can imagine how she was when she came to the center!"

The contrast was amazing. I still shuddered when I remembered what a wretched sight she was a few months ago. "She was the most defeated girl I've ever seen," I said.

Susan came to the center on a bitter cold night in March. She wasn't more than a handful of brittle bones and I'll never know how she made her way through the fierce wind that was blowing. But somehow she got to our front door and when she found the bell she leaned against it with her whole body. That's the way I found her when I opened the door.

She was shivering so hard that she couldn't talk and I helped her into my office where a fire was burning. Carmen had come downstairs to answer the bell and she ran for some blankets. We tucked them over the thin, shabby coat the girl wore.

A half hour later she should have been warmer, but she shivered worse than ever. Carmen had rubbed the color back into her hands, and when the girl began to moan I thought she was feeling the pain of the blood beginning to circulate through her fingers.

Then I knew I had to take a closer look at her eyes because I began to realize what was wrong.

They were all there—all the symptoms I knew so well. The green eyes stared at me dully when I lifted her lids and I felt beads of perspiration forming on her forehead under my hand. No amount of warmth in the room would bring color to that sickly gray skin.

"Do you know where you are?" I asked, gripping her by the shoulders. She nodded weakly and her head drooped to one side. "You're going into withdrawal—do you know what that means?" Again the girl nodded, and out of the corner of my eye I saw Carmen's look of concern.

"Dave! You wouldn't throw her out?" she said.

I couldn't take time to answer Carmen at that moment. I shook the girl again and she nodded.

"If you're looking for a fix, you've come to the wrong place!" I shouted. Her eyes opened and her jaw fell slack and the words just wouldn't come to her lips. I got my answer when a pitifully bony hand grasped my wrist and I felt the ragged fingernails dig in. She made a tremendous effort and spoke two words in a voice I could barely hear—"Help me!" She didn't say another word for two days.

Carmen really believed I would have given Susan back to the wind that night if she had come to us by mistake. But I had to find out whether Susan wanted a bed for the night or hope for her soul. It was even more important for her to know what she wanted.

The next time I saw Susan she was exhausted but able to talk. In fact, she was very willing to talk about herself. She spoke in a strange, monotonous tone, as if she were telling a story about a girl she hardly knew. She was such a quiet girl, such an unprotesting victim—perhaps aloofness was the only way she could hold onto the threads of her sanity.

Susan wasn't a run-of-the-mill addict. She was the only child of a decent, respectable family; she was also a deserted wife and an unfit mother.

She didn't get hooked as a teen-ager. Oh, some of her schoolmates smoked marijuana and a few sniffed heroin, but Susan would have no part of anything like that. She was a good student, and when her father died her mother took a job as a typist so that Susan wouldn't have to drop out of school. Mother and daughter were very close and after Susan graduated from high school she got a job in her mother's office. She was an excellent typist and a conscientious worker, and the two women began to enjoy a pretty good living.

Then Susan met Mike. A friend introduced them and Susan thought she was in love with him from that moment. Her mother didn't like Mike but her objections only seemed to make Susan determined to prove them wrong.

Susan and Mike got married and they were quite happy until Susan became pregnant and had to give up her job. Then their money didn't seem to go very far and Mike began to come home later and later. After her daughter was born, Susan tried to close her mind to the suspicion that was beginning to haunt her, but her friends let her know what other people were thinking.

"You gotta face facts, hon," was the advice of her best friend. "Mike's got roving eyes and he's making the rounds of every girl in the neighborhood. He even made a pass at me. I tell you this for your own good."

Susan was a soft person, and a cruel barb could work its way deep down into her soul. She said nothing to Mike and she let her friends rattle on, but inside she ached.

All too suddenly the rumors and gossip became facts in a much uglier picture.

"He didn't come home one night," Susan said, "but I was used to that. Then a cop came to the door—it was the middle of the night and he woke up the baby when he banged on the door.

"The baby was screaming in the bedroom and I just stared at the cop while he told me Mike was in jail. Mike was with another woman when they arrested him—the cop told me that, too."

"Why was he arrested?" I asked, and when she looked at me I saw that she had never recovered from the shock of that night.

"He was a pusher," she said, as if that were the last thing in the world I would suspect.

She had never suspected, but that wasn't strange. Mike was in the narcotics racket strictly for profit—he was too smart to get hooked.

Mike didn't want his wife to see him in jail and he went off to serve his sentence without a word of goodbye. Susan was too dazed to protest. She knew she had to think about supporting herself and little Janie and she went about making arrangements with a peculiar air of detachment. Her old boss was glad to get her back, Janie began to spend her days in a day care center.

Susan saw a lot of her mother again and was thinking of moving in with her when a visit from an old friend of her husband turned her life into a nightmare.

Harry was a pusher, too, but Susan didn't know it. She thought he was a nice guy who was looking out for his friend's family. But Harry wasn't clean; he had an expensive habit and he was looking for new customers.

Like sharks, pushers can smell blood when a soul is wounded, and Harry sensed that the quiet, lonely girl was having some rough moments.

"I felt sorry for him," Susan said. "He told me he was hooked, but it was a long time before he ever let me see him take a shot. One day, when he did, I got curious. He looked so peaceful when he was high—I wanted to have that kind of peace!"

It started with one little shot—"just to see how it feels." Soon she got to shooting it up on weekends; then she wanted it every day—and never did she find the peace she sought.

Harry had been very generous. He had paid for the fixes and bought the liquor they drank before they went through the ritual of the needle. Then, abruptly, he cut off the supply.

"I thought he was kidding, at first," Susan said, shaking her head. "He said I'd have to buy my own stuff. I laughed. I didn't believe I was hooked." She closed her eyes but the memory was locked inside her. "He was horrible! He smiled and sat down. He said we'd wait and see what happened." Quiet, gentle tears fell from the closed lids. "He didn't have to wait long. After a few hours I would have sold my baby for a fix!"

Susan sold everything else during the next few years. Her habit raced ahead of her salary, so Mike got her into a new profession—prostitution. For a while she tried to work at both jobs, but her fingers could no longer find their way around the typewriter keys and she lost her office job.

Janie suffered more than anyone. Susan often forgot to take her to the day care center and the child was alone in the filthy apartment most of the time. Underfed, unwashed, unloved, Janie cried herself into rages that attracted the neighbors' attention, and when Susan came home one afternoon she found the apartment empty. The police had taken Janie to a shelter and Susan's mother was trying to get custody of the child.

"Mama didn't know till then how bad I was," Susan explained. "I tried not to see her when I looked real bad, but I think she had some ideas. She tried to help—she'd give me money so I could eat and I'd spend it on the first fix I could find."

There are years in Susan's life that she will never remember clearly. She remembers the terrible routine she began to follow, day after day, but she cannot account for many of the hours in those days.

To cut down on expenses, she got a cheap room in a rundown Brooklyn slum. She slept late in the mornings and kept a bottle of whisky on the floor by her bed for those wrenching moments when she awoke. If she couldn't afford whisky she bought the cheapest wine she could find.

Her working day didn't begin until the early evening—unless she was out of little white packets—and she spent most of the day drinking herself into shape for it. Then she hit the streets to earn her living, and by that time she needed $100 a day to keep from screaming.

"I just didn't care," she said. "I didn't even care enough to die. Once I was sitting at a table, drinking, all by myself. I never had money for the electric bills and I burned candles most of the time. All of a sudden I passed out. The next thing I knew, I woke up in a hospital with burns all over my face and no hair on my head. They told me I fell right into the candle and never woke up. It was a neighbor who found me and called an ambulance—and I hated her for doing it because I had to go cold turkey in the hospital. But they gave me some medicine to make it easier."

And when she got out of the hospital she headed for a fix.

Susan learned about Teen Challenge when she passed some of our workers at their street corner services. Sometimes, on her way to "work," she would stop and listen to former addicts describe the strength and help they found in the Bible. Now and then she passed the center on Clinton Street and lingered for a moment outside the iron fence, wondering whether she would ever have the courage to go in. Addicts had to go through cold turkey if they went there—and no medication, either. No, she couldn't go through it, not without some kind of help.

Maybe she could just cut down on her habit—get it under control. Sure. Why not? Then she could shoot it up now and then and really get something out of it.

It didn't work, and the habit increased. The more Susan tried to cut down, the more she thought of nothing but that needle. In her anxiety she almost killed herself with an over dose and again she found herself in a hospital ward.

When she was released that time she felt she deserved a treat. Her mother had given her money to pay her rent for another month, but Susan gave her last cent to a pusher and splurged on two little white packages which she put in her pocket and fingered lovingly as she headed for home.

In her room she prolonged the preparation of her injection, luxuriating in the sight and smell of the powder as she "cooked" it up and sterilized her needle. She waited too long. As she lifted her arm she clenched her teeth at the sight of all the scabs and scars. Her other arm was just as bad and she didn't have time to look for a vein that wasn't blackened and useless. Desperately she jabbed at her arm and bit her lip to hold back the cry of pain that came to her lips. She jabbed again, blindly, and leaned back against the wall as she felt the drug entering her bloodstream.

Still holding the syringe in one hand she slowly let her body slide down along the wall to the floor, where she remained for several hours like a spectator in a boxseat on the pit of hell.

Susan was a little high when she went out that evening. She was saving the other envelope for later—she would need it if business was good.

Down on the corner a group of Teen Challenge workers had set up a microphone and one of them was talking to the small crowd who gathered around, some to laugh, some to stare, and some to weep. They were bad for Susan's business, but she had time on her hands and she stopped to listen.

The boy at the microphone turned in her direction and

seemed to be speaking to her. "You junkies are the biggest fools in the world," he shouted. "I ought to know—I was a mainliner not very long ago. I know how you tell yourself you'll kick the habit tomorrow, or the next day, or when something special happens. But you'll never do it!

"You're the biggest suckers in the world, too. You let the pushers take every cent you've got—and you cross your fingers, hoping they didn't cut the white stuff too much this time!

"You kid yourselves most of all! You say you can't go cold turkey—well, it hurts but it won't kill you! You go through a lot worse pain worrying where you'll get your next shot!"

*This isn't my night!* Susan thought in disgust. She turned away from the crowd but the voice followed her along the street. "You say you can't straighten yourself out—but you can hit people over the head or sell yourself on the streets, can't you?"

Susan hurried down the street until she couldn't hear the stinging words. She was too shaken to work the street without another shot to boost her and she went home to use her second envelope.

This time she was in no mood to make a celebration of it and she gathered her equipment quickly, standing impatiently over the burner.

While she waited she remembered the dirty little girl in the hall and for the first time in many months the thought of Janie passed through Susan's mind. She tried to remember how her daughter looked. How old was Janie? Susan's hands flew to her temples and pressed hard. How old was anyone?

She ran to the bureau and wiped her hand over the clouded mirror propped up against the wall. She was horrified by her reflection. She looked very sick, very, very old—but she couldn't remember her age!

"I knew I had to do something right away, or I'd never do it," she said. "It was no use telling myself I'd do something tomorrow."

She started to collect her pitiful belongings, but it took too much time. She knew she would be lost if she stayed in that room with the burner for another minute. She took her coat and put it on as she ran down the stairs to the street.

Allen and I got wrapped up in the problems of running the school, and the afternoon flew. I hadn't planned to stay for supper but I couldn't resist the invitation.

The dining room was formal and gracious and it brought out the best in the girls. In fact, the dignity of the entire house was a form of rehabilitation in itself. Voices that once screeched "Fink!" above the traffic in the street now came to my ears in the gentler tones of conversation.

I hadn't seen Molly for hours and I was about to accuse myself of neglecting her when she sat down across from me—but not before I noticed something different about her. Her skirt no longer fit like an onion skin, and although she had a lot to learn about sewing, the effect was remarkable. I said nothing and neither did Susan.

My idea hadn't been wrong, after all. Molly and Susan would be good for each other.

I had a lot to think about on my way home that night, so I didn't mind driving alone.

I had given Susan some advice before I left, but I wasn't

sure it was the best kind. She was beginning to think about the practical problems in her life, and there were many.

Most of all Susan wanted to be a mother to her child. That would take a lot of time and much of it would depend upon Janie's response to a mother she remembered with fear. But before Susan could begin to work on that problem she had to consider how she would support her.

She could always go back to a job as a typist and she could earn a good salary, but that wasn't what she wanted. Susan was like a lot of our converts. "I want to tell people about God. I want them to know that Jesus isn't just a name. And I want them to know about the power and strength the Holy Spirit can give them." Her voice was still such a small one but her intensity would carry her words to the ends of the earth.

"Some people won't want to listen, Susan—maybe lots of them."

The obstacle I had thrown in her path didn't even slow her down. "Then I'll just keep talking. Somebody will listen—I did once."

Maybe I did the wrong thing, but I guess I'll keep on doing it. I encouraged her. In fact, I promised to help her prepare for Bible School.

I couldn't bring myself to encourage her to go back to a job that demanded nothing but nimble fingers. Susan wouldn't make much money in a career of searching for God's lost children, but she didn't want to get—she wanted to give.

Boredom was one of the most common elements in the lives of young people who got in trouble. Life didn't ask enough of them. That's why we weren't surprised when converts wanted to come back and work on the Teen Challenge staff. It wasn't easy for them to find jobs where they could really use themselves—and we needed all the help we could get.

Some people raised an eyebrow when they learned that many of our workers were the spawn of the streets—former addicts, muggers, rapists, prostitutes. *Were these people qualified to work among the lost?* they asked.

Yes! And they have the only qualification that counts—redemption!

Who can help an addict as well as another addict who had been saved? Who else really understands his kind of hunger pangs? And who else can tell an addict—in his own language—about a Saviour?

Susan and Molly were two entirely different personalities, but their experience in suffering had given each of them a training nothing else could match. Sin was real to them and they had lived in its slime. When they accepted Christ as their Saviour, and when their lives were cleansed through His forgiveness, they not only knew what it meant—they *felt* what it meant!

The rain had stopped about an hour before and the setting sun was trying to break through the gray clouds for at least a moment before it set. It succeeded for a few brilliant seconds and the whole valley on each side of the highway sprang to life in deep reds and purples. I had to squint my eyes against the sudden brightness.

Then the sun set and darkness came on quickly.

In a way, I too was trying to break through the clouds in my mind, and I felt a strong need to pray. "Lord," I said, "let Your light shine in my mind and help me to see clearly. There's so much to be done and I don't know what should be done first."

One of the clouds on my immediate horizon was a pretty desperate need for supplies at the girls' school. I had noticed the shortage of chairs—any kind of chairs—and some of the girls sat on the floor during classes. Allen wasn't a man to complain, but he needed some basic things such as knives and forks, lamps, sheets, and pillowcases.

I had planned to go out with Billy and Joe that night to hold a street-corner meeting, but they would have to go without me. My time had to go into finding some money.

I told myself that I was putting first things first, but apparently I wasn't very convincing. That discomforting question began to prick away at my mind again. *Was I responding to the right need?*

It was time for me to come to grips with that question.

# 6

My wife has four young children who come to her with their problems. She certainly didn't need mine. So I decided to talk to another minister—my mother.

I found her down in Washington Square the next evening. It was the first time I had gone there to hear her preach and I decided to watch for a little while.

It was almost dusk and a warm breeze was blowing the grit and papers along the ground. The little park in the square was crowded with people, most of them very young, who arched their necks in the breeze. Some of them sat on benches—carefully avoiding any vacancies on the benches by the checkerboard tables. Only the hicks would have taken those seats—and they would deserve every bit of the fiery wrath that would fall from the lips of the old checker players who had squatters' rights there.

I saw my mother and Fay Mianulli talking to three young men near a water fountain. They didn't use a platform or a microphone and from my distance they looked like a group of neighbors discussing the season. I had to get very close before I could hear them.

"What exactly do you know about the Bible?" my mother was asking one of the young men. He was tall and very thin and he bent over her, with his head to one side. He pulled thoughtfully at the saddest, scrawniest beard I ever saw.

My mother looked up and smiled in my direction but not at me. A policeman came from somewhere behind me and walked up to her with an almost theatrical look of disapproval on his face.

"Mrs. Wilkerson," he said, as if he were about to scold her, "I thought I told you people you couldn't give a lecture in this park without a permit."

My mother's smile grew as he spoke. "Officer, we also agreed that I don't give lectures," she said politely.

"All right—sermons, then," he said, folding his arms across his big chest. He was so much taller than she that his chin rested on his collarbones when he looked down at her.

"Officer, I'm not breaking any rules—you'll see that if you join us for more than a minute." She turned to the thin young man who was trying to turn his face away from the policeman. "This young man and I were having a conversation. He knows me and stopped to ask me a question. I am in the process of answering that question—and possibly asking a few of my own." She waved her arm to include the fairly large crowd that had gathered behind the policeman. "Now, if these nice people are interested in our conversation and want to stand close by so they can hear it, is that against the law?"

My sympathies as a man were with the policeman—he didn't stand a chance. But as a fellow minister I rejoiced in that woman!

The policeman had his own problems. A smile was tugging unmercifully at the corners of his mouth. "All right, Mrs. Wilkerson—just don't overdo it," he said. "This crowd can get pretty rough."

As soon as he walked away Fay moved into the crowd and began to hand out some pamphlets. Some of the people were too curious to refuse them, but a few pulled back in fear. "Are you a bunch of Communists?" one man said, insinuatingly. He stood near me and I was about to answer for Fay—not that she needed it—when a tall, very beautiful blond girl in front of me turned and scrutinized him as though he were some kind of insect.

"Watch your tongue, mister," she said in a deep husky voice. "These are God's people." She was provocative and threatening at the same time and the angry questioner was confused. He looked around for a sign of support, but all he got was a snicker. He turned and pushed his way through the crowd. The girl laughed louder than anyone. There was a spatter of applause and she bowed to acknowledge it.

Fay smiled at me in greeting as she turned to the girl. "One of these days you're going to mean those words, Betty," she said casually. The girl had fooled me—I thought she was serious.

"She's just one of the crowd," Fay told me when I asked about the girl, "but she's always here in the evening. I haven't given up hope for her."

The girl wasn't quite typical of the usual Village beatnik. She was trying to appear stark by doing without makeup and letting her straight hair hang along each side of her face down to her shoulders, but there was a certain neatness about her clothes that didn't fit the rest of the picture. Her companion was something else.

I watched Betty stroll over to a sullen, dark-haired woman who carried a huge guitar on a strap around her neck. She seemed to be all beatnik—dirty, ragged jeans, black sweater stretched out of shape, and sneakers held together with knotted shoelaces. From her haircut I wasn't even sure at first she was a woman. But her face softened as Betty approached, broke into an ingratiating smile. I couldn't hear what Betty was saying, but it was obvious that she was giving orders. It was also obvious—painfully so—that the woman was eager to obey. I watched her dig into her pockets and pull out cigarettes and matches, almost dropping them in her haste. Nervously she lit a cigarette for Betty who seemed to take a cruel pleasure in the other woman's clumsiness.

The distaste growing in me must have showed in my face. I was always appalled by these obvious, unnatural liaisons.

"Yes, she's one of them," Fay answered before I even asked the question.

"And you still have hope for her?" I said.

"I have hope for everyone, Dave," Fay said. "And especially for Betty. I think she might be a normal girl, but she's so terribly mixed up. She's tried all kinds of things—Zen Buddhism, hypnotism, psychoanalysis—and now this."

"What's she looking for?" I asked.

"The same thing they're all looking for—help," Fay said, matter-of-factly, and I realized why my mother could work so well with this remarkable woman.

I turned as I heard the chords of a guitar. Betty was sitting up on the back of a bench, tuning the guitar, and several people stood around her. She strummed a few more chords and waited for absolute silence.

Her low honeyed voice seemed to come up out of the earth itself, softly at first and then increasing in volume with each line of the song she sang. As she strummed she kept time by thumping the heel of her hand on the body of the guitar, and before long she had the onlookers clapping their hands to her rhythm.

*Got no more home than a do-og,*
*Got no more ho-ome than a dog;*
*Well, I lost every friend I ever had.*

My mother had come over to stand beside me. "Don't you wish we could put a gospel hymn in that girl's heart?" she said, and I understood. Betty was singing a bitter hymn to misery, the story of her life. She was so effective that I could feel myself flinching as the song went from verse to verse. If such a talent could sing of joy, of a fresh, clean life, what might happen in the hearts of her listeners?

"You're winning me over to your side," I said—but that wasn't news to "the Beatnik Preacher."

Thinking about Betty's problems made me forget my own. I remembered my reason for going to the Village while I was driving home. It was just as well—my mother had enough on her mind.

I should have gone straight home, but something pulled me toward the center. Things were quiet there. Billy had taken Vic to a street-corner meeting. Mario was getting ready to go to the farm the next day, and even the dormitories were settling down early.

Maybe I wanted to wait for Vic to come back—I wasn't sure. Vic had been at the farm for eight months and now he had come back to the city for a few days—"just to see how it feels." I knew what that meant and so did Billy—that's why he wanted to go along with Vic to his old neighborhood.

There was always one last reservation in the mind of a boy who used to be a gang member—and Vic was certainly one of the worst of them. Did a Christian have any guts? Vic had to find out. He had done well at the farm. He liked to work with the new arrivals and his enthusiasm for the Bible seemed to catch on with them. But Vic was beginning to wonder whether he was using the farm as a hideout.

"He's going to test his guts," Billy said when he brought Vic back from Rehrersburg.

He was testing mine, too. Anyway, something was keeping me at the center, and I gave in to it. I called Gwen and told her I would spend the night there.

I should have known better than to question the feeling I had. I was needed at the center that night.

It was late when Al Lorenzo came and he brought his nephew with him. He didn't call before he came—I guess he was afraid I'd find some new objection.

According to Al, Greg Lorenzo had finally stopped lying to himself. "He told me tonight," Al said. "He knows what he is—and he wants to change." He slapped the tall, good-looking boy on the back.

I had my doubts, but not for long. A few minutes later I was absolutely sure that Greg wouldn't go through with it. He wasn't high, but the effects of his last shot hadn't worn off completely. He was much too cold to mean anything he said.

I could imagine what had happened. The boy didn't want to hurt his uncle but he wanted to get him off his back. So he was trying to humor him. Maybe he had begun to realize that addiction wasn't a joyride, but he wasn't ready yet to get out and walk the long distance home.

Al didn't see it. He had worked so hard for this moment that he couldn't believe it wasn't the real thing.

I'll say this for Greg—he was the most immaculate, and the best-dressed young man who ever walked into the center, including the staff. His clothes were expensive and I wondered how he ever made enough money to support his habit and his taste. I knew that homosexuals were willing to pay well for the kind of favors he no doubt provided, but still—

I decided to wait. Greg was beginning to plot the distance between his chair and the door. While Al talked I kept an eye on the boy.

I didn't have to wait long. Al was telling Greg about the farm when the boy suddenly stood up. His body was rigid and only his eyes moved.

"It's all right, kid," Al said, taking him by the shoulders and trying to ease him back to his chair. "You knew this would happen. We'll see you through it."

Greg wrenched himself free, and the carefully combed waves of brown hair fell across his moist forehead. He reached to his neck and pulled at his tie and when it wouldn't loosen he ripped at it until it hung like a waiting noose down across his chest.

He looked to me for support. "Tell him," he said, pointing to Al. "Tell him I can't do it—not even for him!"

Al was confused. "He's not ready yet, Al," I said. "You pushed him too hard. He thought he'd shake you once he got here. But you stayed and he couldn't get out!"

"But I would have found out about it—that doesn't make sense!"

"Addicts never make sense. They don't think—they just crave."

"Why can't you crave something decent?" Al cried. He seized Greg and shook him violently. The boy didn't resist. His head snapped back and forth until Al let him go.

"I'm going out that door now," Greg said to the big man who stood helplessly in front of him, his chest heaving up and down, "I don't want you to follow me—not now, not ever." His voice rose in anger. "This is my life I'm living and you've got no place in it!"

"I'll stop you," Al said. His voice was low and he didn't raise a hand, but his determination seemed to fill the room. "You meant what you said tonight—I know you did! You're sick to death of your rotten existence!"

The boy said nothing. He smiled at a joke he alone enjoyed.

"You remember—when you were a little boy I used to tell you about Jesus? When your father used to shoot it up and you were afraid to stay home with him, you'd come running to my house—remember? And I used to tell you to run to Jesus that same way—"

"Knock it off!" Greg snapped and turned toward the door.

"He can do more for you now than I ever used to do," Al went on, ignoring the boy's remark. "Nobody else can heal you, Gregory—but you've got to go running to Him, real fast!"

Greg's hand was on the doorknob. He slammed his fist against the door. "Cut it out! Cool that Jesus stuff—you sound like a nut!"

"So—what do you care? I'm just a stupid old man!" Al dropped to his knees. "Look, kid! Look at the crazy things I do! I even pray!"

Greg opened the door but he couldn't leave. He crouched in the doorway, trembling, and shaking his finger at his uncle. "You're a creep! Do you hear me? A crazy old creep!"

Al bowed his head in prayer. "Jesus, Jesus, care for this boy and follow him wherever he goes. Don't let him rest until he gives himself up to You." Greg stumbled over to Al and in his rage he held his fist over his uncle's head. But Al didn't stop. "I can't keep after him any more now, Lord—but You can."

Greg wanted desperately to hurt his uncle. "I hate your lousy Jesus!" he screamed. Then he stopped, shocked by his own words. Al was silent, too, but only for a moment. When he spoke his voice pleaded, "Forgive him, Jesus—that's not really the boy talking."

I thought Greg was going to smash his fist down on Al's head and I jumped up to stop him. I was mistaken.

I had seen a lot of the sordidness in the life of a boy like Gregory Lorenzo. Some of it was beyond my imagination. The facts alone would make most people sick but Greg seemed to be hardened to the worst kinds of ugliness and depravity. Yet the sight of his uncle—powerful enough to have crushed the boy who cursed his God—kneeling in humble prayer, and asking forgiveness for him, was the thing that broke the boy.

Greg's features twisted as though he were in pain and with a great dry sob he threw himself to the floor. Al reached out for him hesitantly. "O Jesus, open his heart to Your love!" he whispered.

I was kneeling, too, and my prayer mingled with Al's. I had drawn the line at Gregory. Fortunately, God ignored it.

"He can't help me," Greg said. "I'm not like these kids—I'm worse than that!"

"Ask Him, Greg," I said.

"He can't—I'm rotten!"

*"Ask Him!"*

He could hardly lift himself up on his knees. "Lord?" he said, in the doubtful tones of a child opening his eyes in a dark room and calling for his father. "Lord?" he called again, a little louder.

I watched his face as he lifted his head and I saw a smile of surprise and happiness. "Lord!" he said in a strong, clear voice and clasped his hands together. "Show me the way!"

Later that night Al and I watched Gregory fall into a deep sleep. Even though the boy's face had relaxed, the hard lines of suffering were still visible. I was glad—for his sake and Al's—that he seemed to be having an easy time in withdrawal.

Greg had spent a long time in the chapel where other boys were unburdening themselves to God. He heard about lives that matched his in wretchedness and he listened to boys who had begun to walk in a new way.

"Funny how they always cry when they give in," Al said to me later.

"That's when they really see themselves for what they are—sinners." I said. "Most of them think *sin* is a pretty cute word—until they look at it from God's point of view. It crawls and it smells. That's when people understand how much help they need—and that's when they cry."

"It always tears me apart," Al said.

"I know. But it's got to happen—or they'll never be able to realize how much God loves them. First they have to see how hard it is for anyone to love them."

The night didn't end for me when Al left. It was 2 o'clock in the morning and Vic wasn't back yet. Billy was still out too, so I assumed they were together—at least that's what I wanted to assume.

Billy knew what Vic had to face. When Billy had gone

back to his old turf to preach the love of God, he got a knife in his ribs. Vic had been a vicious little punk before his conversion and lots of other little punks had scores to settle with him. They wouldn't have tried anything in the days when he carried a knife—but now he carried a Bible.

I tried to concentrate on a sermon I had to prepare, but I looked up at every squeak in the house. Every time the front door opened I went into the hall to see who came in. I began to feel foolish as well as anxious.

It was nearly 3 o'clock when I heard the front door open and recognized the voices of Billy and Vic in the hall. I tried to slow down as I reached the door of my office but I couldn't conceal my relief.

Billy's face was pale and Vic seemed shaken, but they were all right! Late as it was, I could see they needed some coffee and we all went to the kitchen.

Vic had been through a critical night and he had gone through the worst of it alone. He and Billy had stayed together during the street-corner service. There were some hostile threats from a gang of Vic's old friends who stood around the platform, but Vic stood his ground at the microphone. "You can't count on the gang any more," he said, holding up his Bible. "This is your best protection. The gang is falling apart—the needle saw to that."

The boys grumbled a bit but they didn't start any trouble. After the service they drifted away and Billy and Vic began to pack up their equipment. That's when one of Vic's old friends stepped out of a darkened doorway and called to him.

"This guy didn't run with the gangs—he was a loner," Vic explained. "I knew he didn't want to fight. But he was the guy who got me started on H."

The boy looked so sick when he walked under the streetlight that Vic felt sorry for him. "He wanted me to take him home—he looked too weak to make it by himself." So Vic took him home—to a shabby room on the next block—in spite of Billy's objections.

"I no sooner got him in his room and he dove for the mattress," Vic said. "Then I knew what was up. He was trying to stretch out his supply because he was low on dough—that's why he was sick. And there I was—an old customer!"

Vic was reliving the awful temptation right before my eyes. Normally his blue eyes protruded slightly but the strain that sucked in his cheeks made them look very prominent. He drummed on the table with both hands.

"He pulled out a couple of sticks of pot from the mattress and handed them to me," Vic continued, wiping his hand across his brow. "Dave, I thought I was comin' apart—right on the spot! I wanted to reach out and grab them, and I hated myself for it. I pushed them away, and this guy reaches under the mattress again and pulls out the prize—the little white bag!"

Billy got up angrily. "Why didn't you get out—then? You can't handle that kind of trouble!"

"Don't I know it!" Vic said and he turned to me. "That's what saved me, Dave. I remembered—you said we shouldn't rely on our own strength, and that's what I was tryin' to do. So I decided to ask the Spirit for some help."

"Did you get it?" I asked.

"Yeah!" he said, still a little awed by it. "No loud noises, no lightning, nothin' like that—but my hands got steady and there was a good feeling inside me. I felt real quiet again. I looked at that white bag and I didn't want it. That's when this guy gave up tryin'. I think I shook him up a little, too!"

"That's not all, Dave," Billy said with a grin. "Vic tried to bring his friend here."

"Why not?" Vic said, taking him seriously. "Anyway, I got him to take a card with our number on it. He might use it someday."

I remembered a card I had once given to Vic. He didn't use it for a long time but when he came to the center at last he gave it back to me. It had been handled so much that it looked like a piece of cloth. It was also full of irregular lines and creases—he must have crumpled it up in anger more than once. But when he needed our telephone number, he had it.

Now I looked on a stocky, tanned boy who was strong in spirit as well as body. Addicts don't stand up well under pressure, but this former addict had faced a crisis that night. It taught him that he could resist a powerful temptation.

Vic hadn't really needed me that night, but I was glad to be there. Sometimes I got tired of hearing myself tell these kids that they had to stand on their own two feet and face their problems. But every now and then I had a chance to see one of them do it, trembling knees and all, and that gave me the stamina to keep after a hundred more kids.

Billy sat up with me for a while after Vic went upstairs. It had been a busy night and I wanted to relax before trying to sleep. I told Billy about Greg Lorenzo and he was just as surprised as I had been.

"Did he tell you about Rose Martinez?" he asked.

"No, what about her?"

"She's branching out. She's moved a couple of prostitutes into that old building."

Billy had seen Rose a few days earlier when he was visiting a boy who had been caught in another raid on Rose's shooting gallery. Rose looked so bad that Billy couldn't get her off his mind. He wanted me to go and see her.

"Sure, I'll go, Billy—but just to talk. We can't put pressure on a girl like that or we'll lose her completely."

"But she looks like death now! She must be shooting it up to the limit!"

"And loving every minute of it! We can't get through to her yet, Billy. She probably gets her supply for nothing and she's undoubtedly the most business-minded junkie in town. I don't know if she'll live long enough to get desperate."

"That's what I mean, Dave."

I shared Billy's worry. I felt that way about every kid in trouble. So many times I had tried to look after the ones who didn't respond to an offer of help, but early in my mission I had to make a choice. I could lose myself in a thousand dead-end lives or I could try to put a few of them on the road to God.

Still, I tossed a lot that night. I had never seen Rose Martinez, but there she was in my mind. So many terrible things could happen to a girl like her. If she didn't take an overdose one of these days, she might be killed by a desperate addict who wanted to get his hands on some money. And how long would it be before she lost her usefulness as a pusher? She had high connections in the narcotics trade, but they weren't known for their loyalty to a junkie who was slipping.

I finally stopped thinking about Rose—and then Betty popped into my mind. When I remembered her performance in the Square, I smiled because it seemed a bit comical in retrospect.

That thought made me sit up and turn on the light. Was

my mother right? Was I becoming a spiritual snob? I blinked my eyes impatiently. Why did I distinguish between Rose and Betty? Both girls were destroying themselves and who was I to say that one was pretending? Rose was a slum girl and I knew the reasons for her agony. Betty was a Village character—someone the tourists like to see.

*All right,* I asked myself, *which are you?—a tourist or a minister?* There was nothing comical about the beautiful girl who sang so movingly of bitterness, abandonment, and heartbreak. If she used her voice to drown out her soul's cries of pain, she needed help even more desperately than I had been willing to admit.

I turned off the light again and lay back on the bed. I got as comfortable as possible, but I knew very well that I wasn't going to sleep that night.

# 7

I had to travel a lot during the next week, but I couldn't shake off an uneasiness that came over me. I felt as if something terrible were going to happen—somewhere, soon—and I wanted to be there to stop it.

Billy had had a busy week too and he looked very depressed when I saw him again. Rose was on his mind.

I felt too sorry for Billy to say "I told you so." He and Hope Sotto had gone to see Rose one day, fully prepared to have her slam the door in their faces. She didn't. She was very cordial and invited them inside.

"I've been in the worst places," Billy said, "or at least I thought so. But that heap of bricks she lives in—Dave, you don't have to buy the powder to get high! She's cooked so much of it, it's in the air!"

Rose knew a lot about Teen Challenge—she had lost some of her best customers to us—and she listened quietly while Billy and Hope told her why she ought to come to the center. When they thought they had talked long enough, they asked Rose if she had any questions. She did. Did they have any books she could read? They gave her all the pamphlets they had and they were overjoyed when she asked them to come back again the next afternoon.

Poor Billy and Hope. I could imagine how stunned they

were when they realized—several visits later—that this girl wanted attention, not help.

"I don't think she ever gets any visitors—except addicts and the police," Hope said. "We were novelties!"

Rose kept promising to be ready and packed "tomorrow." But tomorrow wasn't on her calendar.

Billy wasn't quite ready to give up. "I want to go back once more," he said, "and I wish you'd come with me, Dave. She might listen to you."

"Don't you see, Billy—she can't hear what you or I or anyone says. The devil's got her ear!"

I knew that wouldn't stop him, and I would have been disappointed if it had. God had called out to Billy for a long time before Billy heard Him. But there came a moment—just a split second—when Billy heard God above the roar of evil that clashed in his ears. And in that fraction of a second Billy reached out and grabbed God's hand and held on.

Maybe Rose had very little time left. But as Billy saw it, she needed only a split second.

My mother usually spent most of her days working at the center, but that morning she hadn't come in yet. I was getting impatient with the problems that were beginning to crowd into my mind and I knew I would see them more clearly if I could talk about them.

I looked in on Gregory Lorenzo and I felt a little guilty about fussing over my problems. They were nothing compared to his.

Greg had been spared most of the physical agony of withdrawal but he was still writhing in his mind. Joe Catessi told me that Greg had gone to the chapel door several times but he had not actually gone inside the room since the night he came to the center. He tried to eat his meals after most of the other teen-agers had left the dining room, and he made no effort to talk to anyone.

Greg was an immaculate boy. His white sport shirt was fresh, his chino pants held a sharp crease, and his hair was neatly combed. His orderliness stopped at his eyes—they were full of turmoil.

Here was a boy who had been hit in the gut and he couldn't get his breath. He had taken a long look at the life he was leading and he couldn't see anything else.

"I can't even get near these kids," he said. "I know some of them, Dave—I'm the one who got them hooked!"

So that was where Greg got so much money! He had started to push—and I could almost guess who supplied him. I was right—Rose Martinez!

"I've only done it for six months or so," Greg said. "My habit was big—and I had a lot of other expenses, too."

A pusher has to build his own business, and there's only one way to do it. Greg began to hang around schoolyards and candy stores. He got to know the kids who had time on their hands and a hunger for kicks.

It cost Greg a few packs of cigarettes, a few glasses of soda, and a lot of hours to build up a complex, profitable enterprise. The kids knew he was good for a cigarette any time and it wasn't long before he flattered them by offering marijuana. Anybody who held back was chicken—and very few did.

Then there were parties for the boys. But strangers began to show up—mostly older men who stood in groups off to one side. They seemed to get their kicks from watching the boys having a good time.

Liquor gradually replaced the soda just as pot had replaced marijuana and the men began to join in the fun. They were very friendly and extremely generous with their money. Most of the boys said they couldn't remember what they did after they got drunk, but some of them felt uncomfortable about it. They didn't feel quite as uncomfortable about their new source of money.

Soon the boys began to buzz about a very special party Greg was planning for them. He was going to show them something new in kicks. Some of the boys didn't like the way they behaved at Greg's parties and they were going to break away from them—right after this one big blowout.

This party had everything—liquor, plenty of pot, the attentive men with money in their pockets, and the needle. Greg's timing was most professional and he unveiled the hideous paraphernalia as if they were the trappings of some ancient demon of darkness. He was very clever that night. He gave nothing away and every packet was sold—the boys were eager to buy and the men were more than willing to give them the money for it.

What a setup! Rose had given Greg the idea—she had a shrewd eye for talent. Greg was already involved with the homosexuals but his habit was outrunning the money they gave him. Rose was always ready to expand her operations, but she was tied down to the shooting gallery—she couldn't trust anyone else with all the money that came in there. Greg's friends liked to meet new friends and Rose was always interested in new customers—Greg could supply both demands.

Greg buried his face in his hands. "If I loused up my own life, that would be bad enough," he muttered. "But it's all those other boys!" He looked up and his tortured face made tears burn in my eyes. "I know what they're in for—I know how they wake up in the morning with a sour taste in their souls!"

Gregory was not a homosexual—I was pretty sure of that. But perhaps he was much worse. He made his living off them. He held parties for them and introduced them to troubled young boys who were flattered by their offers of money and attention.

He knew the vicious treadmill he had led other boys to enter. They would need something to hide behind, just as he had needed it when he began his ugly career. And he gave them over to heroin, just as he had given himself over to it. Then they couldn't run out on their careers because they needed the money for drugs.

Now, when Greg ran into some of those boys, he couldn't face them. "I know they forgive me—I can see it when I get the guts to look at them," he said. "But how can I forgive myself? And how can God?"

"You'll spend the rest of your life wondering how God can do it," I said. "You're not alone there—it makes you just another one of God's children. We all have trouble forgiving each other—and ourselves—so don't wait until that happens in your life." He was so still,I didn't know whether he was even listening to me, but I went on. "Jesus has paid the price for everything you've done, Greg. I know that's hard to understand—especially when you know that Jesus never committed a sin in His life. But that's what the crucifixion means—your debt, my debt, everyone's debt has been paid, wiped out. And His resurrection means that you, I—everyone—can have a new life, a clean life."

"I want to be clean," he said.

"First you had to realize what a sinner you were, Greg," I

said. "But you're not supposed to stay that way forever. God wants you to be a happy young man. He wants you to find out how beautiful your life can be. You've suffered long enough."

He bent his head. "No—I don't think so."

I stood up impatiently. "It's not up to you to make that decision. Your life belongs to God—you don't forgive, He does. You don't pass sentence on yourself—He wants to forgive you, help you. What right do you have to refuse Him?

I took him by surprise. "I'm not refusing Him!"

"Aren't you? Aren't you still holding onto your life right now? If you gave it over to Christ, why aren't you on your knees, shouting with joy because you *are* forgiven?" He couldn't answer. "You're holding out, son!"

I was afraid I had been too hard on him. My own feelings were so strong that sometimes I was carried away by them.

I groped for the words that would straighten his tired shoulders and lift his head. I couldn't find them. We were separated by only a few feet, yet he was slipping far away from me. He had come so close to God on the night Al had brought him in—he had only a few more steps to go, but I was afraid he was going to turn back.

I was preoccupied with Gregory's sadness and I didn't see the girl coming out of the chapel. We ran into each other.

It was Betty, and at first I found that hard to believe. The beautiful, somber girl had been in so many of my prayers and thoughts ever since the day I saw her in Washington Square.

She smiled at my look of surprise. "I came here while you were away," she explained. Her voice sounded tired and then I realized that Betty was exhausted. She leaned against the wall as if she needed its support.

We went into my office and she sank down into the big arm chair. She was hardly the girl I had seen sitting on a bench, singing and strumming a guitar. Betty looked as if she had been very sick—she was thinner and the dark rings under her eyes gave her an expression of wistfulness. Her long blond hair was tied back with a thin ribbon, and I could see that she had a firm, determined jaw.

I noticed something else about her. When I had last seen her, she sent out waves of hostility and agitation. Now I could sense a serenity in her. Gone was the bitterness that had driven her song like a fist into my mind.

I was happy for her. "God bless you, Betty," I said. "You've found peace, haven't you?"

"Yes, she said, curling her long legs up under her and resting her head against the chair. "I've looked for it all my life, without knowing what I wanted. If someone had told me I was trying to find peace for my soul I would have laughed in his face." She looked up with a self-conscious smile. "Or spit at him," she added. "I was a pretty rough character."

Betty had called my mother at the center early in the week. "Please take me in," she said, almost choking with tears. My mother had gone down to the Village immediately.

"What made you come?" I asked.

"It rained one night," she said and I waited for her to go on. She was so lost in her recollection that she forgot I was listening. "I'm sorry," she said, "I keep reliving that night—I hope I always do."

My mother and Fay didn't go to the park when it rained, but we had had a dry summer that year, and they were in the park every night. Betty told herself that she went to listen to the two women because they were amusing, but when the rain finally came and they didn't show up, she began to face the truth. She refused to turn to the Saviour they preached, but she couldn't live without Him!

"I didn't care about the rain. Something pulled me to the park and I went. I sat on a bench. I sat there all night and I was soaking wet—I didn't realize it."

Betty found what she was seeking. As she sat in the park a feeling of rest and peace came into her tormented heart. "It was time for a fix, and I didn't even want it," she said.

She had tried everything in life—everything distorted, ugly, weird—thinking she needed excitement to keep her going. "I certainly wasn't looking for love—I knew better than that. When I was five years old my father dumped me on a doorstep and drove away. I was so alone, so scared that night—and I never got over it, not until that other night in the rain."

Betty thought she was tough. Nothing could hurt her! First her mother, then her father had deserted her; then she had gone from one foster home to another—abused in the bad ones, too angry to adapt to the good ones. She was put in a correction home for girls when she was twelve!

"I wasn't exactly crazy about women," she said, "but I hated men—with good reason, too." That made it hard for her to go into prostitution when she became a seventeen-year-old mainliner. "There were other ways, though," she went on. "I was pretty and young—and there are women who like to fuss over girls like that."

Betty was convinced that no one cared about her and so she didn't care about herself. She thought she could take anything—the more daring, the more forbidden, the better! How wrong she was!

"The night it rained, I found myself huddling on the edge of the park bench, just the way I had huddled on a doorstep a long time ago. I was scared! And I had been scared all along. I was too proud to kneel down to Jesus—but I needed Him. Oh, how I needed Him!" Betty's voice grew stronger as she spoke and her tired eyes were brighter.

"The rain felt good—it made me feel clean. I couldn't see a single other person in the park, but I knew I wasn't alone. And when daylight came I got up and walked for a long time. The rain had stopped and the sun was shining—and I couldn't go back to what I had been. So I called Mrs. Wilkerson and asked her to come and get me."

I was lost in Betty's story and I didn't hear my mother come into the room. She coughed when Betty finished.

"Now you can help me find that chapel, David," she said. When I looked at her with a big question mark on my face, she explained. "Betty is a convert—you promised to help if I could show you just one."

Betty didn't understand what we were talking about. "If you ever want to go back to the Village, Betty, there might be some work for you to do," I said. "Very important work."

I had stood by long enough while my mother fought a spiritual battle against ridiculous odds. Now it was time for me to pitch in and help.

Before I left the center to go for a long walk in the Village, I telephoned Susan at Rhinebeck. "How's Molly doing?" I asked. She was on my mind, too.

"You wouldn't believe it," Susan said, "but she's showing signs of becoming a popular girl up here."

"Wonderful! How about her classes?"

"She was impatient at first—wouldn't study. She's a lot better now. I think she discovered that the Bible is more than a lot of words."

"And what about you, Susan?"

She hesitated. "I want to write to Janie—she's old enough to read now. I think it would prepare both of us for getting together. I'll talk to you about it when you come up. Are you coming soon?"

"As soon as I can—but that may take awhile."

"I can wait," she said. I hoped I wouldn't have to make her wait very long. My calendar was getting so crowded that I avoided the sight of it.

Dusk was falling over the Village and the night lights were beginning to shine. I had been walking for a couple of hours and my feet hurt.

The real estate agent was about to give up on me. There wasn't much space available on those commercially valuable streets and there was a high price tag on each inch. Even though I knew we couldn't afford some of the rents the agent quoted, I insisted on seeing everything he had listed. He wouldn't have understood my reasons.

Now he limped alongside me, silent and frowing. Occasionally we were separated by the crowds filling the sidewalk.

MacDougal Street was especially crowded and I was rudely elbowed against a low iron railing that saved me from falling into something that looked like a dark pit. A laughing, arm-pointing group of people passed and I saw that they had pushed the real estate agent into the street.

Another cluster of people kept me pinned to the railing while they gazed curiously at a brightly lit shopwindow somewhere over my head. Stores can be found almost anywhere in the Village and the people in front of me were looking at a first-floor apartment that had been turned into an art gallery.

When I tried to squeeze past them I had to turn and look down into the blackness behind me. Something was there—or something had once been there.

As my eyes adjusted to the darkness I could see a few stone steps leading down into a basement store of some kind. It must have been a very narrow one. As I squinted I could see a dirty reflection of my feet in a jagged piece of glass that remained in the frame of a big window by the entrance. I later learned that the glass wasn't only dirty—it was part of a window that had been painted black.

I felt a hand on my shoulder and heard an impatient voice say, "Let's go." I turned and saw that the art lovers had gone and I was free to move—and yet I wasn't.

"Just a minute," I said. "Is this place for rent?"

"You don't want that dive?" the agent said.

"I don't know yet," I said. "Can we go in?"

"I'll have to get a key—it's not my listing," he complained, wiping his brow. When I insisted, he went off to get the key, but I wasn't sure he would come back.

While I waited I went down the steps, groping my way in the darkness. The door was locked and barred by two crossed boards. A few more pieces of wood were nailed up in a haphazard pattern across the open part of the window—the jagged glass on the bottom half would keep out intruders. I could see nothing when I peered through the open spaces.

I felt as though I were standing in a sort of well, with the world rushing by at eye level. It was a peculiar sensation to know I could walk up a few steps and plunge right back into the noise and excitement on the sidewalk. I was ankle deep in old papers, broken bottles, and dirt blown in from the streets, and the building smelled damp and stale. I should have felt uncomfortable in such an evil-looking place, but I didn't. Instead I felt that I was standing where evil had been subdued.

"I'll come right down," my mother said and she hung up without a goodbye. Then I called Fay and got the same response.

I met them outside the basement cafe on MacDougal Street and handed the key to my mother. I saw the happiness in Fay's eyes begin to fade when she looked past me. I had hoped that the surroundings would look better in daylight, but if anything they were more depressing than they had been the other night.

My mother paid no attention to the grime. "I told you, Fay. I said, 'One of these days, David will walk through these streets and the Lord will point out a place for us!' " She led the way down the steps.

Our chapel was to rise on the síte of a former nightclub called the Den of the Forty Thieves—which was evidently as sinister and lurid as it sounded. The room was as narrow as the entrance, but quite deep, and the only window was the broken one in front. In the shaded light that came in I could see more of the details. I was sorry I didn't get the place cleaned up before my mother and Fay saw it.

The floor was littered with garbage, broken glasses, and bottles, and the smell of it told us it had never been cleaned even when it was occupied. What a time the former patrons must have had and what a strange group they must have been! We found a lot of their equipment lying around, most of it broken or smashed, but we were puzzled by some of it. Here and there we found enormous pillows that had been covered with glittering fabrics. Now they were torn, dirty, and mildewed.

Fay had to satisfy her curiosity and she counted the pillows as we explored. "David, there are about forty of them!" she called to us from the back of the room. "One for each thief, I guess."

That explained the peculiar tables we found. At first I thought the legs had been broken off all of them, but evidently the legs had never been more than a few inches high.

Fay was a native of the Village and she knew all about the Den of Forty Thieves. "I heard that they used to lie around on the pillows and watch the dancers—I didn't believe it until now. No wonder the police were always raiding it!"

The Village cafes and nightclubs try to outdo each other in shocking and perverse attractions, but the Den was reputed to be one of the worst. It was not a place for tourists, as were most of the other night spots on MacDougal Street—the Den was a hub of vice for the depraved and distorted.

I began to wonder if I had lost my senses the night I rented the space, and then my mother touched my arm.

"What a wonderful place for our chapel!" she said in a hushed voice. "This is a good start, David! I know it!"

She was sensing what I had sensed when I astonished the real estate agent by agreeing to pay the exorbitant rent for such a "creep joint." God was there and He wanted His lost children to come and pray where they had once reveled.

The back of the room was very dim, but we could see that a kitchen must have been there at one time. We could use the utility pipes and put in some new appliances.

"What about the walls?" I said. They really defeated me. One wall wasn't too bad; it was brick and the messages scrawled on it could be removed with elbow grease and a holy indignation. The rest of the place was designed to look like an Arabian tent.

"We'll need a lot of paint," Fay said. Her enthusiasm had returned and I could see her hands twitching to hold a paintbrush.

"Yes, it's got to be colorful," my mother added. "It's got to make these beatniks feel free to come in and talk—they've got to walk in and see right away that this is their chapel."

Not long ago I wouldn't have believed that such a thing could happen, that such a place could be. Now I knew better. God had pointed out this shabby basement to us, and as the two women talked excitedly about the changes they were going to make I realized that He was about to make His presence known in the Village.

When I got home that night I dropped into a chair and stretched my legs out in front of me. I had that happy weariness that comes to people when they are used by God to carry out His purpose, and my muscles sang more than they ached.

Gwen said that Joe Catessi had called and left a message for me. "He said that he saw Al Lorenzo's nephew go into the chapel tonight—and he stayed there for a long time. Does that mean something special to you?" she said, and added, "Not that I'm nosy."

I couldn't shout my joy because I didn't have enough energy. I rested my head against the chair and closed my eyes. "Yes, Gwen," I said and I reached up for her warm hand. "It means something special for the whole world."

# 8

I saw very little of my mother for several weeks. Every time I caught a glimpse of her there were traces of paint in her hair and on her eyeglasses.

It was early in November and the chapel in the Village would be ready to open in another week. I had just come from a meeting with Walter Hoving, president of Tiffany's and a member of our Advisory Committee, and I went straight to the center to tell my mother the good news. Walter and I had managed to squeeze more money out of the Teen Challenge budget so that the chapel could offer free coffee and doughnuts. "Most of these people don't have much money, David," my mother had said. "They shouldn't feel that they have to pay for their welcome."

I almost fell over some cans of paint in the front hall. If I had complained about it no one would have heard me above the excited voices of the boys and girls standing in front of a huge sign held up by Joe and Greg. The background of the sign was painted bright red, and large white letters spelled out CATACOMB CHAPEL.

"Hey, Dave!" Joe called and the kids swarmed around me, practically carrying me toward their artwork. I could feel their pride and their sense of achievement and for a moment I couldn't say a word.

"Whatta ya' think?" someone called out anxiously.

I looked at all the young faces—some of them still a bit haggard. Most of them had never looked upon a world that invited them to build, to create. They had known only the impulse to smash and run; now they had worked to make something, and they were discovering the anxious joy of standing back to look at it. Their emotions made my words seem inadequate.

"It's good," I said. "It's very good. I'll be honest with you —it's the best sign I ever saw!" A cheer went up and they all began shaking hands with each other.

The name CATACOMB CHAPEL, so appropriate, couldn't be traced back to the inspiration of any one person. It seemed to come from several of us—my mother, Fay, Paul, Joe, and some teen-agers who eagerly took on the enormous job of cleaning the place.

The early Christians in Rome had taken refuge in the catacombs when their lives were in danger; and when I remembered standing down in that dreary well at night I began to see how the chapel might serve as a spiritual refuge for Village beatniks. They would be safe there while the world they feared swirled on the streets above them—and there they could find redemption.

Joe followed me to my office. Something else was on his mind, something disturbing.

"It's Frankie—he's starting to bug me, too." he said, sitting down with a sigh. "I don't know, Dave—he's real trouble for us."

I had to agree with him. Frankie was a problem that wasn't easy to solve. He had looked like trouble from the very first moment he showed up—and he was living up to all our expectations.

Frankie had come to my office about two weeks before

and he practically came right through the door. I looked up and saw a short, heavily built, swarthy young fellow standing in the doorway, his hands on his hips and a cigarette clenched in his lips. He appraised me slowly, along with the rest of the room, and then he stretched out his arms and clamped his dirty hands on the door frame on each side of him. "So, you'd be the director of this joint?" he said with a careful sneer. I didn't know what to expect but I almost smiled—I was sure he was imitating someone he'd seen in a gangster movie.

"Get rid of the cigarette if you're going to stay," I snapped, and I turned my attention to the letters I had been signing when he burst in.

When I looked up, the cigarette was gone. "If you put it on the floor, pick it up," I said. He smirked and reached into a pocket of his worn leather jacket. He pulled out a cigarette with a carefully squashed end. "Waste not, want not," he said softly, sliding into a chair across from me and hooking one heel on the edge of it. "Don't the Bible say that?"

"Why not read it and find out for yourself?" I reached over and held out my hand. "Dave Wilkerson," I said. He looked at me with contempt. I gave him a fair amount of time and when he didn't shake my hand I withdrew it.

"Don't you know my name?" he said. His manner was irritating and my patience was wearing down.

"I don't have time for games, son. Should I know you?"

He sat forward angrily. "Look at me, preacher man! That ought to tell you who I am!" He stuck out his chin as though that would give me a better look at his face and I sat back to study him. The curly black hair, the round, heavily jowled face—and the fleeting sheepishness in the dark eyes! It was

Mario—but a much heavier, more disagreeable Mario! It couldn't be!

He roared with laughter at the confusion on my face. "That's right! I'm Mario's twin brother. Didn't he tell you about me?"

Mario had mentioned a lot of relatives, but only vaguely. He never spoke of a twin.

"I'm sorry I didn't recognize you," I said. "You really look a lot like Mario—but the last time I saw him he was so thin. You're a lot heavier—and healthier looking." The newcomer was full of hatred, too, and that made a difference in his face.

"Where is Mario?" he asked.

Mario was still at Rehrersburg but Frankie found it hard to believe that he was there of his own free will. "You sure it ain't some kind of prison farm?" he said. When I described it to him, a sly look came into his eyes. "He really kicked the habit, then?" he asked.

"So far," I said. "We won't be sure for a few years—but after he leaves the farm we'll keep in close touch with him."

"Will he come back here?"

"Yes, if he wants to. We need plenty of workers."

"That kid!" he smirked. "He's not so dumb, after all."

He stood up slowly and looked around the room again. "Nice joint," he said more to himself than to me. "I wouldn't mind stayin' here myself." He turned and placed his hands on the desk, leaning toward me. "Could I stay here? Just for now, I mean?" He was putting me to some kind of test.

"Do you need help?" I said.

"I'm no junkie," he said proudly, jabbing a thumb toward his chest. "I kicked the habit all by myself—two years ago. What do you think of that?"

"I think it's wonderful."

"I didn't need no help then—and I don't need none now." His manner changed suddenly—he was trying to be very smooth. "But I'd like to look over your outfit. After all, my brother's goin' along with you, so maybe there's somethin' to it. Maybe I need some religion."

"You need God, Frankie—we all do, but we don't always admit it."

"Okay, okay," he agreed. You know best, preacher man. Why not give me a chance to find God?"

I knew he had sized us up as patsies but I let him stay. He didn't need us to help him break his habit—he needed love and care to make him stop hating.

Frankie was the worst guest we've ever had at the center. He complained about everything and he amused himself by starting arguments with anyone he could insult. I sympathized with Joe—and if he was losing patience, how must the others feel about Frankie?

I had delayed sending for Mario because I wasn't sure Mario was ready for a reunion with a brother who had led him along the slimy trails of liquor, marijuana, and heroin, and then called him a weakling because he couldn't break his habit. I must admit that I also thought the delay might give us a chance to get our message across to Frankie.

But it wasn't going to work. Frankie thought he would be able to take us over, and when that failed he got his revenge by making the center throb with antagonisms. No matter how much hope I might hold out for this one sorry youngster, I had to consider the others, too.

"All right, Joe," I said. I'll talk to him and lay it on the line. If he doesn't improve, he'll have to leave—soon."

Joe looked only a little less disturbed. "I know I've failed, Dave, and I don't like it," he said.

That feeling was very familiar to me. "You have to accept your failures in this work, Joe—if you're ever going to have any successes," I said.

I found Frankie stretched out on his bed in the dormitory. I gave him an ultimatum in hard language while he stared at the ceiling, hardly blinking his eyes.

"Okay," he said breezily, when I paused for breath, "I'll square away." He sat up and swung his legs over the side of the bed. "What do I have to do to sign up with this outfit?"

There wasn't a bit of sincerity in his voice and yet I went along with him. "If you really want to sign up for our program, you'll have to be accepted by a group of three people—I'll be one of them."

"Fancy setup!" he snorted.

I sat on a bed facing him. "Listen, Frankie, a lot of people put a lot of work into each kid who wants to be a part of our program. We don't expect guarantees—but at least we like to have some hope for a kid we try to help." I thought he was going to interrupt me but he changed his mind. "Now, it's easy for a guy like you to go around sticking pins in us—and don't worry, we can take worse than that—but it takes real guts to ask God for help."

Frankie shrugged his shoulders. For once he didn't have an angle. "What do I gotta do to be sincere?" he asked grudgingly.

"That's a big question," I said. "I really don't know the

answer." Suddenly I had an idea. "It might help if you could do something that isn't easy for you."

He pulled back slightly. "What?"

There was a Bible on a table near me and I handed it to him. "Take this to Joe Catessi and ask him to mark some Scripture messages in it. Then memorize them—by tomorrow!"

"What for?" he said, looking at the Bible as though it might jump at his throat.

"Well, the exercise might be good for you," I said, going to the door. "And you might learn something."

As I drove down to the Village late that afternoon I realized that I had forgotten something. Billy wanted to talk to me before I left for the Catacomb Chapel and I had rushed off without seeing him.

He probably wanted to talk about Rose Martinez. He still clung to the hope that he might be able to slow her down in her mad race toward destruction. It was useless. Rose was getting bored with visitors from Teen Challenge.

Rose was one of a growing number of problems that had to be left hanging in midair. My schedule was getting even more complicated and I was still trying to find the reason for the strangely alarming depression that frequently came over me.

The first thing I noticed about the chapel on MacDougal Street was the clean sparkle of it. The thick drift of paper and dirt had been cleared out of the entrance and the well around the steps, now the few papers and old leaves that blew in found nothing to keep them there. They circled around as if they were trying to look in the new glass window—and then, distressed at what they saw, they rose in the air and danced hectically down the street.

The day was very cold and I was glad to get inside until I realized that the basement wasn't really warm. The only source of heat was an electric room heater and that didn't go far.

Nobody else seemed to notice the chill. They were too busy scraping, painting, scrubbing. My mother and Fay couldn't stick to supervising and they pitched right in with the heavy work, enjoying every minute of it.

The change in the room was incredible! It was no longer an imitation of an Arabian nightmare. It didn't look like any chapel I had ever seen, either.

The brick wall had been left as it was, except for a good scrubbing, but a work of art had been performed on the wall facing it. It had been a depressing concrete wall covered with dark glossy paint, but now it looked like another wall of bricks. They had been painted on!

My mother had told me they were going to paint the ceiling black. It sounded like a terrible mistake but I had to admit that it looked good. It gave the room a warmth and intimacy that overcame the chill of a basement atmosphere.

Mother had found some old wooden tables and an assortment of chairs. They were scratched with names that had been worn almost smooth with time, but they were a great improvement over the pillows and low tables of the Forty Thieves.

Betty was there, working with a paintbrush, and she put me to work rubbing polish on the tables. I was glad to see that she wanted to work in the chapel—it wasn't easy for her to come back to the Village.

"I didn't want to come, at first," she said as she painted the final "brick." "I was afraid to look at what I had been. But I learned something here—if I hadn't come back to look my memories in the face, they would have come after me." She glanced at the door as it opened and a tall, thin boy stepped inside, uncertainly.

He was a beatnik—or at least he wanted to look like one. His clothes were baggy and dirty but his long sideburns and tapered beard had been trimmed with great care.

My mother had seen him, too, and she greeted him from her perch on the ladder. "Come in," she called. "We're not officially open yet, but you're welcome."

Confusion crossed the boy's pinched face as he looked around. "I thought they were kidding me," he said to himself. "Are you really going to pray here?" he asked my mother.

"I certainly will," she said with a soft chuckle. "And I hope a lot of other people will, too." Then she became serious. "What about you? Do you ever pray?"

He shifted his weight to another foot and looked away from her. "What do I have to pray about?"

"You're alive, for one thing, and you might thank Him for that."

The boy looked at my mother as if she were a nice little lady who had pushed the wrong doorbell.

"He's an addict," Betty whispered to me.

"Are you sure? From this distance?" We were standing across the room from him.

"You can't see it, Dave," she said, biting her lip. "Only people like me can understand that kind of language."

Like most beatniks, the boy wasn't dressed for winter. His black sweater was thin and his jeans were worn. The bare ankles above his sneakers were almost blue from the cold.

He muttered something to my mother and walked over to the electric heater where he stood rubbing his arms.

For some reason I couldn't go back to work on the tables. I felt the boy's eyes on me but when I turned around he wasn't looking at anyone in particular. He was watching all of us with an amused smile—but his eyes weren't laughing. They saw something else.

Maybe I could understand the kind of language Betty mentioned! Something in this boy's eyes matched the uneasiness I had felt for weeks. It wasn't a cry for help. It was something much fainter.

I left the can of polish on the table and didn't even take time to say goodbye. I had to get to my car and pick up Billy and Hope at the center.

Rose was the reason for my depression, for my conviction that something or someone needed me! I was accustomed to hearing the shriek of a soul in desperate need of help—but for weeks I had been hearing the pitiful, silent plea of a soul that was too weak to reach out for anything.

I didn't care about rules, or principles, or the probability that I was on a wild goose chase. I just had to get to Rose and there wasn't time to wonder why.

Rose Martinez lived and did business on one of the darkest streets in Brooklyn. Most of the buildings had been condemned for one reason or another and no one seemed to think of any better use for the property. A lot of the street lights had been broken and no one came to repair them.

We pulled up in front of a darkened building that looked just like the others—I couldn't see a single light anywhere.

But Billy knew where we were going and I didn't question him.

He led Hope and me around to a door in back of the building. It was heavily boarded. Billy ran his fingers along one of the boards and pressed a small button I never would have noticed. Nothing happened for a few moments.

Then I saw a sliver of light through a crack in the door and the door swung out toward us, boards and all. Whoever arranged the secret entrance was quite clever—he never disturbed the boards designed to keep people out.

I couldn't see who was holding the flashlight on us and when I heard a voice I wasn't sure it was a woman. "Well, surprise," I heard, and the voice was so hoarse that my own throat felt sore. "You brought a friend!"

We walked in and followed the flashlight deeper into the building until we came to another door. Beyond it were all the comforts of an addict's home.

There was a lot of furniture in the room—the big, thick, overstuffed kind—but everything was faded, stained, threadbare. There were no windows but this part of the building had electricity, plenty of it, and lots of outlets along the floor. A pile of hot plates and candles were stacked on a chipped, scarred table in the middle of the room.

Rose followed us after carefully closing and bolting all the doors as she went along. She padded into the room and I finally got a look at the girl who had haunted me for such a long time.

She was a tall girl, very stoop-shouldered, and she shuffled her feet along the floor as she walked. Her skin was drawn so tightly over her bones that it made me catch my breath—the bones looked as though they might pierce the skin at any moment. Perhaps that was why she moved so carefully, so slowly. She was wearing a wide sleeved, Oriental type of dress which made her seem even more angular.

The face above the long, thin neck was like some kind of primitive mask. No light found its way into the deep hollows where eyes and cheeks hid, and the only expression was a streak of bright lipstick that stretched into a mocking smile.

"Don't bother," she rasped in that painfully hoarse voice when Billy began to introduce me. "I know him—I know all you finks." She threw her head back to get a better look at me through her half-closed eyes. "You're putting me out of business!"

"I wish I could have done it sooner, Rose," I said. "It's killing you."

Rose was dying of malnutrition and I doubted that she could remember the last time she had eaten. She had forgotten food. All she wanted was a fix and when she got one she began to think about the next one. I could see that she was in a terribly weakened condition. The shuffling walk, the careful gestures, the slow speech—none of it was an act. They were genuine symptoms of a body that was down to its last ounce of energy.

Her angry outburst had winded her and she leaned heavily against the table. "That's the whole idea," she drawled. "Death is the last fix—the last and the best."

Billy held out his hand. "Come with us, Rose," he said in a choked voice. "You shouldn't die before you know what it is to live."

"Don't be stupid!" she laughed, waving her arm in a limp circle that was meant to include her whole world. "I've really lived! I got everything—I'm a rich woman!" She turned to Hope who stood watching her, unashamed of the tears on her cheeks. "You—you're a good kid, but you won't let me do something for you," Rose said. She straightened up suddenly. "Wait! I'm not going to be around much more—I want to give you a present for being so nice to me." She stumbled to a door that opened into another room. When she came back she was carrying a fur coat. She held it out to Hope who shrank back from it.

"Here, honey," Rose said, trying to force the coat into Hope's arms, "it's yours. When can I use it? I can't ever leave this place—and soon I'll be out of business. Take it!"

"Oh, Rose," Hope sobbed, "I don't want the coat. I want you to come with us."

Rose threw the coat on the floor at Hope's feet. "You want it, all right," she sneered. "If these finks weren't here, you'd take it!"

Hope tried to reach for Rose's hand, but Rose spun around toward the table. She gripped the edges and stood looking down at the horrible assortment of eye droppers, needles, bottle-caps, hot plates, rubber stoppers, razor blades.

"This is my god," she said, and her shoulders heaved up and down as she struggled to get her breath. "He's given me lots of coats like that—money, too. I've even got some jewels stashed away." She turned to me. "My god lets me fly out of this lousy world whenever I want to. And soon he'll take me out of it for good." She stretched an emaciated arm toward me. "Now—what can your God give me?"

"Your god has made a fool of you, Rose!" I said. "He's sucking your life out of you, one needle hole at a time. What about all your money? Can you go out and spend it? Can you trust anybody to take care of it for you?"

She turned away from me. "You came at a good time—

business gets good at this time of night," she said, as if we had just come in.

I took her arm and turned her around gently. "Rose, you asked me a question about God—the only God. He can give you life—the only life that means anything!"

"I don't want to live!" she shouted. "I want to die, die, die! That's all I've ever wanted." She wrenched away. "I tried so many times to kill myself with an overdose—it never worked out right! Somebody always came in and pulled me out of it. But not this time—I'm so shot up I can't even get high any more!"

"Why do you want to die?" Hope asked.

Rose laughed bitterly. "Nobody ever gave me a reason to live."

I knew what I had to do. "Rose," I said, hardly believing the confident tone of my voice, "my God can give you a reason. If I can prove that to you—tonight—will you come with us?"

"You're crazy!" she said.

"Will you come?"

She let herself fall back against the table and stared at me. "All right," she said quietly. "Let's see you go into your act."

I could feel the trembling in my legs and I sat in one of her filthy chairs. "It's not an act." I looked at my watch. It was 10 o'clock. "Let's wait for another hour. You said your business is good around this time of night, so let's give it a chance. But if no one comes to that back door in an hour, you'll have to take that as proof that God is a good reason for you to live."

Billy and Hope were stunned but Rose smiled. "You've lost, already," she said. "You'll hear that buzzer any minute."

"How about it, Rose? Will you let God prove His love for you?"

"Sure, sure," she said, easing herself carefully into another chair. "I can't lose."

Each minute was an agony. So many times I thought I heard footsteps somewhere outside the building.

We had only ten more minutes to wait and that was when Rose began to get nervous. She got up and paced until she was too tired to walk another step. When she sat down she ran her hands through her hair.

I began to feel calmer. "Thank you, Lord," I prayed.

Billy marked the end of the hour with a great sigh and Hope threw her arms around Rose. "Get some things together," Hope said. "I'll help you."

Rose looked like a rag doll that had been tossed aside by a furious child. I didn't think she had the strength to stand up and I took her hand and helped her. Her bright, shiny mouth was slack and she shook her head in disbelief.

She looked around the room at all the riches she had looted from the souls of other miserable young people. As Hope handed her the coat that had been lying on the floor, Rose put out her hand to stop her. "No," she croaked, "I don't want it. I don't want to take anything with me."

We left by the back door and Rose stopped for a moment. She ran her finger along the boards and found the hidden buzzer. She pressed it and we could hear it ringing inside.

I realized what she was thinking. "Yes, Rose. It was working all the time," I said.

# 9

I knew Rose could get through the physical part of withdrawal. Her system had absorbed such a heavy amount of drugs that withdrawal pains often began to set in soon after she took a fix.

Her spiritual exhaustion worried me. Could a girl with such a strong will to die give herself over to a will to live—and in time?

Hope refused to leave her side. She sat up all that night reading the Bible aloud.

I spent a lot of time in the chapel. Rose had opened my eyes and my heart a little more and I felt very humble. Everything I had said about addicts and the desperation they had to feel was true—but I had to follow God's will, not my rules. Sometimes an exception came along and I had to be ready for it.

The world of sin that Rose had known ever since her unwanted birth had so weakened her spirit that it could not even cry out in a voice that man could hear. But God heard it and He nudged Billy and me until we finally went to answer it. No wonder I had been troubled by a feeling that something was going to happen!

I prayed for Rose, and I prayed that God would always poke me in the ribs whenever I listened to my own voice instead of His.

I had said enough to God. I knelt in silence so that I might hear anything He wanted to say to me.

Several people had passed me in the chapel but I really hadn't seen them. I looked up quickly when I heard someone cry out, "Mario!"

Two boys were a few feet in front of me. Mario was kneeling and Frankie crouched beside him. "Mario!" Frankie said again, as if he couldn't believe what he saw.

Mario had put on some weight and I could see that he was indeed Frankie's twin. He smiled at his brother. "I'm real," he said, putting an arm around Frankie's shoulder.

"You don't look the same," Frankie said. Astonishment had wiped out his brashness and I saw friendliness in his face for the first time.

"I'm not the same, Frankie," Mario said. "You were right. I didn't have any guts—not like you. But I'm stronger now, Frankie. I'm not on the needle."

"I heard about that—I'm glad for you, kid." Frankie shook his head—that was the most he would give in to emotion. "You got the real guts, kid—not me. It ain't enough to break the habit. I think about going back on the needle every minute, every hour. What about you?"

Mario beamed. "I'm free, Frankie! I never knew what it was to be free until now! *I don't want the needle.* I want to stay free!"

Frankie was silent. He crouched closer to the floor. "This is a nutty place," he grumbled but Mario didn't hear him. He was praying aloud for his brother. "You're one of them!" Frankie whispered, suddenly aware that other people could hear him.

Mario went on praying and his voice was joined by others in the room, all praying for Frankie.

I looked at the belligerent little hoodlum who had tried to scramble up my life, and I prayed, too.

Frankie couldn't take it. If we had shaken our fists in his face he would have loved it. His muscles were made stronger by hate and he enjoyed showing his strength. But he was driven back to the wall by the honest prayers of kids he had pushed around, insulted, and ridiculed.

"Oh, my God!" he wailed, and he bent his head. In a voice heavy with tears he began to recite, "Give us help from trouble: for vain is the help of man"—a verse from Psalm 108!

On and on he went and I listened in amazement. Frankie had memorized all the Scripture passages Joe had underlined in the Bible I had given him—but I don't think he began to understand what they meant until he repeated them in the chapel.

On the day the Catacomb Chapel opened I was packed and ready for a long trip that would take me to some of the Teen Challenge centers in other cities. My plane was to leave early the next morning.

Everyone was busy. I said good-bye to Frankie and Mario before they went to the farm and that got me off to a good start.

The twins had a lot of catching up to do. The terrors of the slums had driven them closer together than most brothers until their lives began to deteriorate. Eventually they came to hate the sight of each other—probably because they had to see themselves when they looked at each other. Frankie thought he was king of the world because he had locked himself in a room until he kicked his habit—but one look at Mario told him that it wasn't that way at all. One weak moment, one little pressure, and he'd be a junkie again.

Now he looked at Mario's face and saw a strength that he could never find in himself. Mario would show him the way.

Rose was better, too. At least she was sitting up and getting acquainted with food again. I had tried to talk to her many times but she was too tired to say anything. She was so listless. In a way she was suspended between life and death, waiting for one of them to claim her, unable to make a move toward either side.

It would be a long time before she could understand what had happened to her the night she walked out on the needle. She had actually left her life behind in a dirty, old building where the air was polluted with the smell of heroin. Now she was waiting. She had heard about a new life. Would it come?

Yes, it would come, but not for a while. I had never met anyone whose spirit was so undernourished, so beaten, and it would take time to heal. And when her spirit was stronger, Rose would feel it stir within her and she would know a longing for life. And she would reach out for it.

I took Paul DiLena with me to the Catacomb Chapel that night. We finally found a parking space a few blocks from MacDougal Street and walked back, huddled against the November cold.

The Village was having a busy night. In spite of the weather the streets were crowded. Some of the people raced along as fast as they could go while a few determined shoppers shivered in front of store windows.

MacDougal Street screamed with noises. Every time a cafe door opened it let out a sharp volley of laughter—the same kind all the way along the street. But the music varied with each gaudy doorway—drums in savage rhythms, jittery banjoes, voices singing strange garbled words to songs that had no melody.

There was the great big sign. It had looked somewhat awkward in the gracious hall at the center, but it fit perfectly here. As we went down the steps to the entrance we passed three boys leaning over the railing. They were trying to look into the window and they laughed at something they saw. The laughter was like a signal and they began to poke each other in the ribs, doubling up and giggling.

The chapel had been officially welcomed. The new glass window had a big crack down the middle and it hurt me to see it.

Inside every table was taken, so we stood at the door. "I can't believe it," Paul said. "It really belongs here!"

And so it did. It also had the strangest congregation in the world. Very few of them came as couples. Most of them were in small groups of boys or girls and they were dressed to attract attention. The girls wore too much makeup or none at all, and some had smeared thick dark semicircles under their eyes. A few of the boys wore large, comical beach hats made of straw.

It was a self-conscious group. Everyone looked up whenever the door opened and most of them had an almost maddening habit of glancing over their shoulders to see if others were watching them. The laughter was loud but strained and artificial.

They were so young to be so disturbed! Most of them were under twenty—and their attempts to look older only made them look younger. Now I could understand my mother's concern for these kids.

The chapel's work was waiting to be done and Teen Challenge was entering an entirely new atmosphere. These youngsters weren't slum kids. They hadn't dropped out of school and a lot had gone through college. They knew about the Bible, some of them had read it, and a few had even studied it.

These teen-agers had strong feelings about God—they were angry at Him! They blamed Him for everything distasteful about their lives, for every bruise, for every confusion. And they came to the chapel to argue with anyone who didn't feel the same way!

Generally they behaved very well. The NO SMOKING sign was obeyed, giving the chapel the cleanest air in the Village. Some pretty heated discussions were going on over the Bibles on the tables, but I couldn't complain about the language.

I craned my neck to look for my mother and I saw one boy—slight, nervous, and eager for attention—jump to his feet and put a cigarette between his lips. The boy sitting next to him smiled in delight and applauded boisterously.

My mother seemed to come out of nowhere. She called to him from across the room. "Get rid of that cigarette, Tony! You know I won't stand for that!"

The cigarette disappeared immediately. The boy twisted into a mock bow and then he raised his head and lifted his arms. "Praise the Lord!" he shrilled in a sing-song voice of ridicule.

"If that happens again, out you go!" snapped my mother

and she turned her back on him. The boy dropped into his chair as if his body had been weighted. My mother was already seated at a table with a group of girls who began to fire questions at her. She smiled patiently, fingering the Bible as she listened, and before long she had it open before her and was reading it aloud. I watched in amazement as the girls at her table sat forward and listened intently.

"This could be dynamite," Paul said in a low voice. "But Ann Wilkerson is just the right person to handle this crowd."

"It looks that way," I agreed. " I don't think they'd take it from a man—but they'll listen to her."

A folding screen was set up outside the entrance to the tiny kitchen at the rear of the room and Betty came from behind it, carrying a wide tray of coffee and doughnuts. Eager hands reached out and the tray was empty in seconds.

"Hi," she said, coming up to us. "You might get a seat soon, but isn't it wonderful to have a full house?" The happiness in her eyes made her even more beautiful.

Someone else came in and stood near us. I recognized him. He was the beatnik who had come in to get warm.

"I knew you'd be back," Betty said. I realized that she must have talked with him that afternoon.

"I can't stay," he said. He was restless. Even though he kept his hands in his pockets, I could see him clenching them.

"Don't go until I finish my song," she said and she pulled me along with her toward the kitchen. Several girls followed her with their eyes.

Betty's guitar was in the kitchen but she didn't need my help with it. She wanted to tell me about Eddie.

"He came back almost every day this week—he even

helped us paint the kitchen. Dave, I think he wants help. Can he go to the center?"

"Does he want to?" I looked back at the boy. He was watching us.

Betty saw him, too. "I told him you'd be here tonight. I know he'll talk to you." She caught her breath. "Oh, Dave, he's so churned up."

Eddie hadn't been in New York very long, just long enough to connect with the pushers who didn't cut their drugs too much. But he didn't know the city well enough to support his habit by stealing and burglarizing, so he was in trouble.

"I know we can help him," Betty said. "He's not a mainliner yet. He's only been on H for about a year—since his parents died in a plane crash." She saw that Eddie was getting restless and she picked up her guitar.

I stood next to a boy who had lost God and listened to the song of a girl who had found Him. Betty stood in the middle of the crowded, hushed room and I remembered another time I had heard her sing. Now I would hear her fine, low voice sing of joy instead of sadness.

Betty sang with a deep feeling that no heart could shut out.

*Jesus is my shepherd,*
*I am just a lamb.*
*Although I'm not a prize sheep,*
*He loves me as I am.*

Her words reached Eddie and he nudged my arm. "Can I talk to you later?" he whispered.

I felt like singing, too. "You sure can, son!" I said.

On the way back to Brooklyn that night Paul was surprised at my eagerness to go off on my trip. "I thought you were getting dizzy from all this flying around," he said.

"I was dizzy—period," I said. I told him something my mother had said to me some time ago. Her words came back to me all of a sudden one day when I was stewing because I couldn't spend more time at the center. She had told me that I might have to learn to feel at home in lots of places.

And she was right. The center wasn't mine, neither was Teen Challenge. I had a job to do and the time I spent at the center was only part of it.

"We're well organized now and a lot of others are taking up the work I started," I explained to Paul. There were other jobs ahead for me, and wonderful opportunities. Centers like the one in Brooklyn were opening all over the country—more and more kids were going out from them to help their suffering brothers.

I thought of Billy, Jimmy, Sonny, Greg, Vic, Mario, Frankie, Molly, Betty, Susan—Rose would be one of them, soon, and so would Eddie. Many of them had helped each other along the way to God, and I had known so many others like them.

No, it wasn't up to me to pick the place where I would spend my time. Teen Challenge was God's idea and it carried His message—I only made things worse for myself and everyone else when I put my two cents in.

I had been confused by our amazing growth. I remembered wondering whether we were crowding out the Spirit with our file cabinets and piles of paper work. I had seen a lot of miracles happen in the lives of lost kids but I had thought that we were getting too busy for miracles.

How wrong I was! The Holy Spirit was responsible for all our paper work—He was working through us and making us grow so that more angels could be snatched from hell.

All I had to do was open my eyes to the miracles all around me. They were happening one after another, and I knew they weren't going to stop.